SELF

&

I

MATTHEW DE ABAITUA

Published by
Lightning Books Ltd
Imprint of EyeStorm Media
312 Uxbridge Road
Rickmansworth
Hertfordshire
WD3 8YL

www.lightning-books.com

First edition 2018
Copyright © Matthew De Abaitua 2018
Cover design by Ifan Bates

British Library Cataloguing in Publication Data
A catalogue record for this book is available from the British Library

Printed by CPI Group (UK) Ltd, Croydon CR0 4YY

ISBN 9781785630644

'I don't mean to say that books are bad. I mean to say that I have used them like a dope addict.'
Saul Bellow

'I was spark-a-loco the entire time.'
Will Self,
on living with Matthew De Abaitua in 1 Hall Cottages

CONTENTS

NICE YOUNG MAN

For six months in the early Nineties, my employer was the writer Will Self. I worked as his live-in assistant or *amanuensis*, an obscure word that translates as slave-at-hand, a person to take dictation and copy out manuscripts. JG Frazer, the anthropologist and compiler of *The Golden Bough*, also employed an amanuensis after his eyes filled up with blood during a lecture. My appointment was made after a similarly traumatic incident: Will's divorce, and his move out of the family home and into the rented, three-bedroom semi-detached residence of 1 Hall Cottages, Church Lane, on the outskirts of the quiet Suffolk village of Knodishall.

I started work at 1 Hall Cottages on 20 July, 1994, the day before Tony Blair became leader of the Labour Party, and this memoir – the memoir of a literary footnote – concludes with the election of Tony Blair to the office of prime minister three years later. Blair's journey from opposition leader to prime minister was indicative of a cultural shift across these years, a change which moved through our lives as stealthily as a pickpocket.

Will Self was prophetic when he wrote that 'The 1990s will come to be seen as the *Götterdämmerung* of periodicity itself. [N]ever again will the brute fact of what year it is matter so much in cultural terms.' This memoir covers the three years of 1994–1997, a sliver of history suffused with never-againness and no-moreness, and perhaps the last moment in the West to largely evade the digital recording of daily life. It was a time when great parties went untweeted, your relationship status was never updated, and the bleakness of London's municipal parks had to be borne without the soft haze of an image filter. Because I cannot cue up the good old days on YouTube, I am writing this down.

No detail will be too trivial for inclusion in this memoir. Writers tend to be informal – silly, even – when socialising. Seriousness is kept in reserve for the books, for the paid words and august appearances. This is not a biography of Will Self. He appears in it as he appeared to me then: inscrutable, unpredictable, always thrilling. It's a memoir about the ambition of a writer, and that writer is as much myself as it is him. The philosophical and cultural implications of Will Self's work are beyond my purview. I will refer only to his books and articles from this period. The miniature is an appropriate aesthetic. Discussions in 1 Hall Cottages revolved around tiny things – model villages, post-it notes, small jobs. As Will Self has observed, 'you can uncork the meaning of something by using scale.'

In our tiny cottage, enormity resided in the inner landscapes of memory and imagination, and this topography was contiguous with the flat corn fields, the sloping pebbled shore, the slate sea. Our ambitions were equally vast. In fact, as a young man, my literary ambitions were so grand that it's hard to know what might have constituted their fulfilment. The reinvention of the novel? The transformation of the spirit of the age? Or prose that reprogrammed the mind of the reader? If this is a cautionary tale then it is a warning about ambition.

I hold up instances from my life as typical of the pains of an aspiring writer. For my transgressing upon the life of Will Self, I offer the following mitigating circumstances: there is nothing here as personally revealing as his journalism or his novels, when read in totality, or in the sourced gossip of Sunday supplement profilers. Also, it was more than twenty years ago. I am compelled to remember this time while I still can. For once in my life, I want to set things down as they seemed to me at the time. I want to write honestly and risk error, and do so without the greasy, insulating caution that has served me so ill.

There are gaps in my memory. Of course there are. There were gaps in our existence too: daydreams, undistracted afternoons of solitude with novels and something smouldering in the ashtray, the gaps between ambition and the realisation of success or failure. The lost boredoms of yesteryear. I am nostalgic for those gaps. I grew up in them.

Although the memoir covers a period of scant consequence in the florid life of Will Self, it was important to me. My six months in 1 Hall Cottages were rites of the imagination. I emerged a changed man. Not all of those changes were for the better. As Will said to me, over dinner a year after leaving his employ, 'Well, Matthew, what happened to the nice young man you used to be?'

* * *

I am twenty-two years old and my name is Matthew Humphreys. After an unfortunate undergraduate attempt at self-reinvention, some people call me 'Maff'. I am broad-shouldered with large soft hands, perfect for the rugby team, had I gone to public school and not a comprehensive school in a Liverpool dormitory town. I have a puzzle ring on my little finger and a silver ankh ring on my forefinger. Around my neck, tied to a leather strap, I wear some ethnic tat from the accessories counter of French Connection. My outfit is standard down-at-heel student: sixteen-hole Doc Martens, striped Duffer of St George beanie, black jeans, a long black charity shop coat, and wool-lined lumberjack shirts. I have a long-term girlfriend called El, who is also from Liverpool but we haven't lived in the same city for four years.

When Will Self blows through town, I am halfway through a master's degree in Creative Writing at the University of East Anglia, so Will Self is already on my radar. The previous August, I had attended a talk about the comic novel at the Edinburgh International Literary Festival; the panel consisted of Paul Magrs, Professor Malcolm Bradbury (my soon-to-be tutor), the critic James Wood as compere and, at the end of the line, a black-clad Will Self, fitted with a throat mike. As James Wood nervously introduced the talk, this throat mike amplified Will Self's sub-vocal noncommittal snorts.

Afterwards, I stood in Waterstones considering the hardback of *My Idea of Fun*, Will Self's first novel, which had been published with a froth of controversy: a Snipcock & Tweed cartoon in *Private Eye*, and a review in the *London Review of Books* which dwelt indecently upon the photograph of Will Self on the book jacket, the 'author as knowing addict', whose 'cigarette…is held at the precise angle guaranteed to cause the most severe nicotine staining of the fingers.' (The miscegenation of the classes entailed in early Nineties drug culture can be discerned in the social mobility of various cigarette grips – I favoured the old man's pinch-and-draw, the hand acting as a sheltering terrace over the fag, a pose filched from my former workmates on Liverpool docks, who were accustomed to smoking in the wind and the rain.)

I want to dwell on the novel for a moment, before getting on with my own story.

My Idea of Fun was notorious upon publication for its lurid descriptions of psychopathic sexual transgression. Protagonist and narrator Ian Wharton, on being asked his idea of fun by the host of a dinner party, considers an act performed by one of his concealed and rotten selves, wondering how to describe how he ripped away the head of a tramp and then inserted his penis into the 'ribbed ulcerated gullet' of the severed neck; could he describe it in such a way that she could actually experience 'the cosmological singularity' of this horrific act, as if language – artfully deployed – could stand in for reality. He decides that the simile of a mackerel's flesh would evoke the tightly-packed flesh of the severed neck but even such a 'painfully acquired' description would be insufficient. If he confessed his idea of fun, it would become – no matter how horrific or outré – merely another dinner party anecdote.

Ian keeps his murderous self concealed so as not to hurt his wife Jane who is pregnant with their first child. The depiction of necrophilia is embedded in a scene of contemporary middle class domesticity, forming a dark vortex beneath the weary routines of social life. Unlike Patrick Bateman, the lone-wolf protagonist of Bret Easton Ellis' *American Psycho*, Ian Wharton's vile acts take place within the context of the family, and the novel explores the seething tension between a secret life and family life.

Reading *My Idea of Fun* from the perspective of an aspiring writer, Ian Wharton's psychopathic acts are a symbolic disguise for the hoarded grievances and incipient destructiveness of the frustrated author. The act of becoming a writer suggests a violent relegation of the domestic realm, making it subservient to the imaginary. In her novel, *Dept. of Speculation*, Jenny Offill imagines becoming an 'art monster' – the kind of artist who dismisses the good manners of common humanity and takes the kind of individual licence Nabokov exercised when he would not even deign to lick his own stamps. By refusing the demands of the domestic realm, the writer can give themselves over entirely to the needs of fiction. On these terms, striking a balance between the two demonstrates a lack of ambition. It was this kind of thinking that as a young man almost destroyed me, as this memoir will explore.

A debut novel, *My Idea of Fun* dramatises the rites of imagination required in its composition; that is, the rite of passage a prospective author must undergo to write a novel. Will Self's previous book, the novellas of *Cock and Bull*, had featured 'grim party turns' of grotesquerie. The violent psychosexual fugues of *My Idea of Fun* are of a different order. They are preliminary rites auguring a profound metamorphosis of the self. But metamorphosis into what?

Metamorphosis is one way to avoid or deny responsibility. In Kafka's *Metamorphosis*, Gregor Samsa wakes up one morning and discovers he is a giant cockroach (or some kind of vermin or a bedbug: translators differ), and so cannot meet the demands of family and men of business. It is the greatest sick note in literature. Likewise, the metamorphosis of Ian Wharton is intended – like Samsa's – to defy some unwanted obligation.

Ian Wharton is the demiurge of dissociation, a hollow-centred Russian *matryoshka* doll in which various other selves nestle. Faced with the prospect of assuming the mantle of middle-class husband and father-to-be, he is indifferent to it all: he might just as well be 'slumped against the weeping bricks in some shooting alley off the Charing Cross Road'. In other words, reverting to the addict self. Intoxication is a way of blurring the lines so that you are not confronted with the cold hard type of your own writing, and its insufficiencies: speaking of his time as an aspiring writer, Will Self observed that, 'The abyss between my aspirations and what was appearing on the paper was so hideously large that I can relate almost every aspect of my aberrant behaviour at that point to my thwarted writing ambitions.'

Toward the end of the novel, Ian Wharton tortures and disembowels a pit bull then curls himself up into the foetal position to idly fellate its severed penis. Dangerous dog and dangerous dog owner were a symbolic unit on the housing estates of the early Nineties. Such homo-canine eroticism transgresses against exaggerated working-class masculinity just for the hell of it. In the novel, the killing of the dog and subsequent mutual debasement is a preliminary rite to Ian's final metamorphosis.

After fellating the severed phallus of the dead dog, Ian Wharton shambles into town, hauls a passing man called Bob Pinner onto a building site, strips a suit from him, then kills him by gouging out his eyeballs. Ian wears the dead man's suit, parades around in it. He is a sociopath with an unstable or vacuous sense of self, taking on the identity of his victims in an act of sympathetic magic. This play on the mad or bad figure of the sociopath provides cover for underlying anxieties concerning paternity and creativity.

Ian Wharton's crisis is brought to a head by the impending birth of his child. When I ask Will about how he became a writer, he says that he only started writing in earnest after the birth of his children, 'because I realised I was about to be replaced and so better get on with it.' Or as Ian reflects, 'I was certain that the prospect of children, of willing my peculiar characteristics on to a new individual, would force me to confront myself.' Before that confrontation can take place, the unanswered question of the father's self must be resolved: writer or not-writer?

Frustrated literary ambition creates a secret self; the writer-to-be is an arrested imp in foetal position, always self-soothing and self-sucking. The father-as-writer threatens the family, introduces economic instability and rival offspring in the form of novels. A new father becoming a writer is an act of selfishness at the very moment selflessness is demanded. But, unlike addiction, which it resembles superficially in its satiation of a private urge, writing has a claim to a greater good. If the father sacrifices his writing self to fit into a deranged social system, then his paternity will pass that subordination and corruption on to another generation. He will raise another capitalist sybarite, another Fat Controller – the name Ian gives to his demonic mentor and the one who inducts him in his peculiarly talented imagination. His wife Jane is pregnant but it is not Ian's child. Rather, Ian believes the Fat Controller has miniaturised himself, crawled down his urethra, and at the moment of ejaculation, replaced Ian's spermatozoa with his own demonic seed.

The novel twists and writhes against conformity on every level. The reader is flicked repeatedly on the nose to resume their disbelief – as if taking pleasure in the escapist potential of fiction is an act of complicity with a corrupt regime. Unthinking acceptance of the forms and techniques of conventional narrative fiction is congruent with a complacent view of social norms: both are open to debate. What in public may be a sub-vocal noncommittal grunt becomes, in the text, a baroque berating that sews and unpicks fiction and refuses to offer certainty or solace.

* * *

Will Self is one of a legion of writers who visit the University of East Anglia throughout my year of study. The creative writing students attend their readings and jostle awkwardly around the writers, making conversation with them and then destroying it by bringing every promising sally back down to the subject of their own unwritten novels.

This is the price the established writers have to pay for reading aloud from their novels for forty-five minutes. Try reading from your novel for forty-five minutes now without gussying-up your act with a PowerPoint deck or a DJ set and you'll be drummed out of the marquee. In the early Nineties, literature dictated its own terms. So: forty-five minutes of carefully intoned literary prose, ten minutes of questions, and then queues around the block to sign hardbacks.

The university bookshop kept cases of Bulgarian wine for these occasions, and sometimes, if Professor Malcolm Bradbury was in the mood, then he would dispatch me under the tables to open another case, and if the bookshop manager caught me under there, twisting away with the corkscrew from my Swiss army knife, then the Professor would quickly find another conversation on the other side of the room to detain him.

During the Will Self Q&A, I writhe and roil at the back, making my own sub-vocal stops and harrumphs of qualification and disagreement. God knows what they were. It really doesn't matter. I buy the book anyway and offer it to be signed. Afterwards, instead of downing Bulgarian red with Malcolm and the misfits, Will sods off with Terence Blacker, the writer-in-residence, and they tie one on elsewhere.

I head up to York to visit former undergraduate housemates, in the hope of foisting my new status as writing acolyte upon them. They largely ignore me to undertake a two-day amphetamine-and-video-games bender in an attempt to complete the Sega Megadrive game *Kid Chameleon*. On a borrowed mattress, I fizz with sleeplessness, cheap uppers and frustrated egotism, then cross the country by train. Criss-cross. Cross-criss. Reading *My Idea of Fun* until my inner voice takes on some of the novel's scabrous eloquence.

I arrive home in Norwich to a phone call from a friend suggesting I meet her and Terence Blacker in the pub.

I've been awake for forty-eight hours. I should go to bed.

I go to the pub.

Over pints, Terence says that he went out drinking with Will Self. It turns out that not only is Will Self looking for an assistant, he wants Terence to find one from the ranks of the creative writing students, as the position will require a great deal of solitude, and so he thinks it will suit an aspiring writer.

'I'll do it,' I say.

'You'll have to live with him.'

'Fine.'

'In a cottage in Suffolk. It's very remote.'

'I'll do it. I have no other options.'

The job interview takes place during a party at Terence Blacker's farmhouse in Diss. A few of the other students gather there, the ones who like a drink, the ones who – along with myself – form the Creative Writing MA football team. (The team is mixed gender and plays in black polo necks and black track suit bottoms: Terence invited Will Self to join us in a game but he refused on the grounds that writers are not team players.)

A local couple call in at Terence's party. Let's call them Sid and Doris Literary Bonkers. In the *Private Eye* of the period, Sid and Doris Bonkers are recurring characters, the long-suffering and sole fans of Neasden FC, a hopeless football team. Sid and Doris *Literary* Bonkers, then, are the peculiar people who follow the hopeless cause of Literature FC. It's Will Self's term. They are the people who, for want of a better term, I could call the *fucking readers*.

There had been almost no talk of readers at the University of East Anglia MA in Creative Writing. Frankly, in those days, readers got what they were given. Readers were basically *losers*. Now, the opposite is true, and writers are the losers constantly trying to insinuate themselves into the affections of the winners, the readers. (My nostalgia for this period is partly due to the sense that the literary novel was still a force in contemporary culture.) The modern creative writing course includes genre; at its worst, it can degenerate into a debate about whether a sado-masochistic erotic novel featuring unicorns and vampires will sell twice as many self-published ebooks as an erotic novel featuring only unicorns. We didn't have these kinds of conversations in the Nineties. Then, no-one talked about engaging characters, genre, trilogies or – god forbid – whether the protagonist was sympathetic or not. Nor do I remember Professor Malcolm Bradbury puffing on his pipe and opining that what the post-modernist novel required in the post-colonial moment was *more* unicorns. A sympathetic protagonist, an easy and unassuming prose style, and a strong plot – these were marks of weakness. Signs of pandering to the reader. And who wants to hang out with that loser?

After a tequila slammer, Doris Literary Bonkers sits on the laps of the various students, and then becomes over-attentive to me, pawing at my forearm, checking on the solidity of my thigh in a way that makes me realise that she is not merely drunk but having some kind of allergic reaction to the booze. But instead of going into anaphylactic shock, Doris flirts insistently and erratically, spinning through the cottage like a helicopter with a broken rotor. She is so obviously *not-herself* but she will hear none of that sensible talk. With a couple of other writing students, we explore Terence's barn, and Doris staggers out after us. Before I know it, the other students have slipped away, and there in the quiet, dark barn, she makes woozy conversation with me.

'I'm a big reader,' she says, taking a step forward, a step backward. 'Tell me about your novel.'

I nervously explain a novel I am planning about the men who work in a factory raising pigs filled with human organs.

'Oh,' she says, disappointed. 'Science fiction. Why are you writing genre?'

'I want to write science fiction that has none of the pleasures of genre, and all the strangeness of technology,' I reply.

She slurs a question. I ask her to repeat it.

'Why a-fuck you wanna do that?'

I am stumped.

'Whassitcalled?'

'*The Feeders.*'

She looks askance at me, as if my voice is out of tune, then she stumbles backward and grasps my bicep to steady herself. Over her shoulder, lurking in the shadows at the back of the barn, the balding pate of Sid Literary Bonkers gleams briefly in the moonlight.

Doris's wayward manner adds to the faintly hysterical anticipation of our notorious, imminent guest. Will Self *arrives*: six foot five, thirty-three years old and dressed entirely in dilated-pupil black. Light bends towards him like he's a black hole. Terence points me out to Will and I am beckoned over.

We sit at a large round table. Will flicks a tobacco pouch and a large baggie of weed at me and says, 'Make something out of that.'

I make the special cigarette, and thus the first interview proceeds. (The phrase 'special cigarette' is Will's, although I only heard him use it once, when we were on a beach and I was flicking sand with my feet and Will – midway through the act of rolling one – said, 'Please don't do that. You'll get sand in my special cigarette.')

What qualities do I present for the position? I am sufficiently au fait with soft drugs to be comfortable with his narcotic regime, while also displaying none of the signs of an addict to Class A drugs. I have a healthy regard for literature and I can take my booze. What other qualities do I display? I am a nice young man and – oh yes – I am the sole applicant.

Will's senses are attuned to mental illness, whether it's the high-octane whiff of psychosis 'like cat urine', or the 'fateful snicker-snack atmosphere of a closed psychiatric ward'. Having taken a sniff of me, and discovered that I am thoroughly stolidly sane, he moots a second interview. Doris Literary Bonkers makes her way over to Will. He blanks her entreaties, completely disinterested in the reader. Resisting the party's efforts to detain him – drink this, smoke that, let me sit on you – Will Self leaves the party, blinding us with headlights, gravel scuffling from the rear wheels of his white Citroën. We wave goodbye until we realise how uncool it is.

Terence's cottage is large. I crash on yet another borrowed mattress, my head a waltzer, the tequila and the marijuana the mischievous lads who leap on the back and give the cars an extra spin. Around and around the oily night I fall, spiralling down into fathoms of dreamlessness.

* * *

The second interview takes place in the cottage Will is renting in Suffolk. He collects me from Saxmundham station in his white souped-up Citroën. He rarely drives now, I believe, for philosophical reasons, but I wonder if this decision owes something to the four or five occasions that he nearly killed us in that car. On the drive to the cottage, he changes gear the way a singer goes up an octave: as an intensifier. The car provides him with an angry voice with which he conducts an unending and furious argument with the system – the system being, in this case, the tedious conformity of traffic that keeps everyone alive.

I am attempting to make intelligent conversation when – for reasons neither of us can quite fathom – Will puts his foot down to overtake a hay wain on a blind bend. Loose strands of hay escape their bales and whip in through the open window. My fingertips prickle. Who or what waits for us on the other side?

Open road. Close one, though. Close enough to warrant a remark, if not an apology. Will mutters something about taking it easy.

I have brought with me a copy of William Gaddis' *J.R*. A truculent post-modernist, Gaddis had recently visited the university, and so Terence and the other staff were obliged to read his difficult novels. Terence did not put up much of a fight when I offered to borrow William Gaddis' *J.R*. I and a couple of my fellow students dallied with experimental literature – Raymond Roussel, Raymond Queneau, Pynchon, Burroughs, Boris Vian and André Breton, the *nouveau roman*, and bloody William Gaddis, in town to promote – no, entirely the wrong verb, he was in town to *warn us* of the approach of another impregnable vessel of his prose – the jauntily-titled *A Frolic of His Own*. In person, it was clear that the frolic was not autobiographical.

20

Gaddis had the curmudgeonly turn of an ignored genius. He was a living warning against taking the experimental path. If Gaddis felt he was ill-served in life, it is for the best that he did not survive to see his legacy played out in Amazon reviews (to quote: 'Will I read Gaddis again? – hmmmmmmmmmm, maybe I'll just stick pins in my eyes') If experimental fiction is read at all, it is as an act of nostalgia, a let's-pretend that we live in a bygone age of progressive culture, in which today's formal innovation will inform the mode of tomorrow. Or to recapitulate a lost era of difficulty as a rebuke to the present. The lot of the literary experimentalist is satirised in Martin Amis' *The Information*. I think Gaddis' way of interweaving voices was on Amis' mind when he devised the scene in *The Information*, from Richard Tull's experimental novel 'Untitled', in which 'five unreliable narrators converse on crossed mobile phone lines while stuck in the same revolving door'.

Anyway, as opening gambits go, for a job interview with a writer like Will Self, packing Gaddis is a sound one.

Will asks about the Gaddis as soon as I am through the door. 'What's it like?'

'Difficult. Like an echo chamber of different speakers and you have to discern who is who by their rhythms of speech. Not entirely rewarding.'

'I haven't read it,' he says. 'He's the one I've never got around to.'

'I think that'll be on his gravestone: "Here lies William Gaddis, the one you never got around to." You can borrow my copy when I'm done,' I say, joining a long tradition of readers keen to hand on the obligation of Gaddis.

The interview is conducted on deck chairs in the back garden of the cottage beside the rusting frame of a greenhouse. We begin by shooting whisky bottles with an air rifle, then follow up with the special cigarette. And how am I to interpret the air rifle? Male writers and their guns: Hunter S Thompson, Hemingway, William Burroughs with his William Tell act. But this is an air rifle, such a diminished phallus to wave around when compared to the lethal members of the American literary tradition. Will takes deliberate pleasure in this irony.

With the informalities out of the way, Will lays down the responsibilities of the position of amanuensis: I am to acquaint myself with the *oeuvre* – not merely his works, but the works that he will be writing about. I must read the library of influential literature in the study, and related works concerning drugs, psychoanalysis and anthropology. Secondly I can bring no Class A drugs into the house, nor am I permitted to drink more than the government-recommended twenty-four units of alcohol a *day*. I am to do whatever I am asked. Nothing is beneath me: laundry, transcriptions, fetching and carrying.

'Any questions?' he asks, observing the standard form of the interview.

'Do you want some more of this?' I ask, handing over the special cigarette.

I get the job. I am to return to Norwich to tie up my affairs and then, in a couple of months, he will come in the Citroën to collect me.

I ring my girlfriend El to tell her. She is pleased. It will be an adventure, and that's what she wants for us. She is not ready to go back to Liverpool. It's still a recession out there. We've come this far on our wits. Why stop now?

AMANUENSIS

The cottage is one of a semi-detached pair of worker's cottages, and in no way bucolic. We park on a track that runs between wide flat fields and 'a liner-shaped copse' (as described in Will Self's short story 'Flytopia'). The rippling wheat-field is a deep pile of soft, closely-packed fibres. The hedges are bursts of thorn and tangle obscuring a drainage ditch that runs alongside this divot in the landscape that I am about to call home.

We go through the small gate. The long grass in the back garden is scorched, brittle and ochre. Pushing its way between the flagstone and the neglected turf, a single opium poppy lolls under its own heady weight.

Will crouches down, and dents the pale papery head of opium with his forefinger.

'Fucking ironic,' he says, walking on.

'What do you mean?'

He disappears into the house.

The front room is his study. It contains a desk, a selection of adored typewriters in their sheaths, a wheezing Amstrad word processor and printer with the special box of printer paper, a fax, again requiring its own particular stationery, and then the bookshelves, one of which is occupied by various editions and translations of his own books: the debut short story collection *A Quantity Theory of Insanity*, the novellas of sexual transmogrification *Cock and Bull*, and the debut novel *My Idea of Fun*, largely represented on this shelf in the scarlet-trimmed, card-covered Atlantic Press edition.

The flock wallpaper is obscured by yellow Post-it notes on which he has scrawled gnomic images, observations, commandments, themes, characters. I've never seen a work-in-progress exteriorised in this way before: the aide-memoires, the prompts, the grit about which the imagination accretes. Post-it notes because their weak glue allows them to be easily reconfigured, for images to agglomerate and overlap.

The living room is small and bare with no television and no furniture. Two dozen coils of flypaper hang down from the ceiling, each riddled with flies. Most are dead, but some flies are still alive, and struggle against the gum. The previous winter, the drainage ditch which runs alongside the cottage flooded, and sludge seeped into the house, seeding the walls with fly eggs. Now it is summer and the eggs have hatched.

I put down the box containing my stereo and watch a fly hop up a strand of flypaper, using the backs of its gummed comrades as stepping stones. Upon discovering a still-living fly, the liberated one buzzes furiously in an act of rape.

'No, not rape,' says Will. 'Look more closely. Its proboscis is going into the chink between head and thorax. It is feeding.'

'Fucking 'em and eating 'em,' I whisper.

We stand quietly in the empty fly room.

'I want you to buy a sofa for here,' says Will. 'As cheap as you can find.'

This residence, temporary and rented, will be appointed for functionality, containing all that we need to write, and nothing more. No distraction, no adornment, no bloody television.

He shows me the six bin bags containing his possessions, ransacked before taking leave of the family home.

'I want you to unpack these bags,' he says.

'What if I come across anything private?'

'It's *all* private, Matthew. I'm trusting you. I can't unpack them. It's too painful. When you've left a family like I have.' He leaves the thought there, and I am too young to know if it is complete or incomplete.

'Buy a filing cabinet,' he says. 'And organise it all. White folder for personal and driving-related material. The red folder for work. The folder with the black trim for money.'

The kitchen is a narrow galley. On top of the empty fridge, there are vials of oils in which strange shapes float. A twig of rosemary intertwined with oregano floats like a spinal column with attached nervous system: flavoured olive oils bought by his girlfriend Victoria from Selfridges Food Hall. Something luxurious.

Will shows me a tub of Lavazza and the coffee pot.

'Fresh coffee goes in here.' He holds up the pot.

'Used grains go in here.' He holds up an old Lavazza tub.

'Why do you keep the used grains?' I ask.

This question rattles at the bottom of a deep well.

Upstairs, he shows me my room.

'There is no bed. Not yet. I ordered one but it won't arrive until tomorrow. You can sleep in my bed tonight.'

'I… I…'

'I won't be in the bed, Matthew. I'll drive to London and sleep there.'

'I couldn't possibly. I'll sleep on the floor.'

'Take the bed. *Mi casa, su casa.*'

I've never heard this phrase before.

He translates for me, 'My house, your house. I will drive to London, to Victoria's place, and then bring her back tomorrow. You'll need some money for a bike and things. Start sourcing what we need. I want bunk beds too, for the kids when they visit. Linen, pillows, and a duvet for yourself. And an axe for chopping wood. There is a long list. We'll go over it tomorrow.' He hands me a hundred quid.

'Get receipts for *everything*.'

I make us some coffee, storing the used grounds as per instructions. We drink it while admiring the flypaper. And then he is gone, and I am alone with the flies.

The next morning, I walk the mile or so into Leiston. I buy a racing bike advertised on a card in the newsagent window. Fifty quid. Then onto the hardware shop for the axe. Figuring that if there is wood to be chopped, I will be doing the chopping, I drop twenty-five quid on a good axe. I make enquiries about the bunk beds then ride back down the Saxmundham Road, feeling pleased to have discharged two of my duties. I return to the cottage to find the heavy ironwork of my bed delivered out front. I haul it upstairs, assemble the bed, drop the axe off in the shed, then ride out to the ruins of Leiston Abbey.

As an undergraduate, I had enjoyed a peak experience in Fountains Abbey on a summer's day. On the way in, under the growing influence of LSD, I had a difficult encounter with a trickster travelling with a troupe of Morris dancers. Crouched beneath a black cloak, he hopped around like a giant crow. In lieu of a head and a face, he had a bird's skull attached to a set of long straight wooden jaws. I tried to walk around him, not looking too closely at the elongated skull, but he would not let me pass.

Clack-clack-clack went his wooden beak. I guessed he wanted money but I had none to spare. Crouching low, shuffling the cloak around him as if it were feathers, the figure hopped convincingly from one leg to another and repeated his demand.

Clack-clack-clack.

I had one pound fifty in my pocket and needed every penny to pay for my entrance to Fountains Abbey.

'Look,' I explained, 'I appreciate that you are playing the role of a trickster, and cannot break character by speaking to me like a man, but you must understand I cannot give you any money because I need it all to get into the abbey.'

Clack-clack-clack.

The inside of the wooden tongue was amber. The ornamental gardens of the entranceway blurred as they began their giddy ascent. I smiled like a big normal person. The previous time I took LSD, I had a nasty vision of jaws inside a dark hood, and ran around keening, quite unmanned, for five minutes or so. I had forgotten all about *that*. I didn't want to get the fear again. Or worse, the state of mind known as the *vibe*. Will teaches me the hierarchy of dread: after the fear comes the vibe, and beyond the vibe there is only the *heeb*, and not many people come back from the *heeb*. (I will later use this riff in a short story, thus adding a definition of 'heeb' to the eighth edition of *Partridge's Dictionary of Slang and Unconventional English*. As far as I know, nobody ever used these terms for the hierarchy of dread again.)

I smiled and nodded at the birdman, and through clenched teeth, I made him an offer.

'I'll give you a quid if you'll fuck off,' I said.

Clack-clack.

Was that assent? I dropped my money into the wooden jaw and then hustled through the turnstile after my friends. The rest of the day was eminently pleasant. We frolicked with peacocks and listened to sackbut in the cloisters. We hid during closing time so that we could have the place to ourselves, sitting at various meaningful junctures in the ornamental water gardens.

Remembering these halcyon days of undergraduate youth, the bygone never-to-be-recovered events of *last summer*, I sit alone in the ruins of Leiston Abbey and try to feel artistically juiced.

The next day, Will returns in the Citroën with Victoria. Her dark hair is short to the nape of her long neck, and she is wearing a collarless V-neck dress, buttoned down the front, red with curlicues of indigo and orange patterning. Her fringe is brushed back, and she will often fiddle with it, self-consciously smoothing it over her ears.

Victoria has a flat beside the Thames in Hammersmith. (I cite this London district now, aware of what it signifies, but then I was ignorant of the London metonyms.) She works as a reader for a television producer, scouting for books that are suitable for TV adaptation.

Not that we watch television in the cottage.

We drive out to the sea front at Aldeburgh. Will barters with the fishermen in their huts and secures the biggest lobster in their catch, a baleful blue monster that they keep around the back of the hut in a tin bath. We sink a pair of pints while they kill it for us. I carry the lobster, warm and wrapped in newspaper, to the car. It has the armoured heft of a rocket launcher.

Back at the cottage, giddy with first-night excitement, Will and I take turns to pose deadpan in the yard with the lobster on our shoulders. Oh lobster, dear lobbie. Symbol of the Surrealists: Dalí's lobster telephone, or Gérard de Nerval walking his lobster Thibault at the end of a blue ribbon in the gardens of the Palais-Royal, asking why was it any more ridiculous to walk a lobster than walk a dog, or a cat or a gazelle?

The lobster, dredged up in its pot from the depths of the unconscious, is a symbol of the dreamworld, strange and out of place in our conscious realm. But not upon the dinner table. On the dinner table, the lobster appears entirely at home.

I am dispatched to the big house of our landlady Mrs Franklin to borrow some implements for cracking the lobster. I am not without some below-stairs skills: I make fresh mayonnaise and fry some courgettes. Victoria lays the table, serves the good wine she has chosen (Victoria always presides over the wine and thinks nothing of sending two, three bottles back to the cellar if they do not meet with her approval). Will stakes out the table with tall candles. At dusk the candles are lit, the lobster cracked, and we gorge ourselves upon it. It is a good evening.

A breeze through a half-opened window riffles the Post-it notes in the study. On the desk, there are cassette tapes of a conversation between Will Self and JG Ballard. The Amstrad whirs and Wordperfect awaits.

Transcribing the interview between Will Self and JG Ballard is my first major task as amanuensis. Even though the commission is only for a brief interview and profile in the *Evening Standard*, the transcript is very important to Will, as it covers his first meeting with one of his literary mentors.

I will try to make a distinction throughout this memoir between 'Will', who is the man who walks around the cottage and employs me, and 'Will Self', the author. I do not want to presume particular insight into the literature of Will Self merely because of my familiarity with the biographical ephemera of the cottage. He made it clear to me that the reputation of 'Will Self' could be used to draw attention away from his private life. I will uphold this division because it is indicative of the Chinese walls in a writer's heart.

Undertaking the transcription, I also bring myself up to speed on Ballard's novels: *High Rise, Concrete Island, The Atrocity Exhibition, The Drowned World, The Unlimited Dream Company,* and the new one, *Rushing to Paradise.* In my headphones, I listen to Will Self and Ballard (later known to Will as 'Jim') discuss the nature of their respective literary imaginations. Ballard's imagination is speculative, 'forensic': he writes as if performing an autopsy, exposing the innards of the human condition from a position of emotional and professional abstraction.

'My emotions remain uncommitted to whatever my imagination happens to generate,' says Ballard, with theatrical dispassion.

Ballard's autopsy of social norms is disassociated in tone. The 'psychopathic hymn' of his novel *Crash* concerns the sexual pleasure of car crashes, set out in dry, patient prose. Ballard rose to prominence as a science fiction writer and *Crash* was written against the prevailing mode of science fiction at that time, with its claims of rational extrapolation of possible futures. He was not interested in being mechanically predictive, but psychically so, anatomising future psychological pathologies arising out of the collision between our selves and our machines.

Toward the end of the interview, Ballard and Self discuss the deleterious effect of the car windscreen and cinema screen upon the imagination.

Will Self says, 'People of my generation are afflicted with this as if it were a virus; they are not aware of the extent to which their view of their own identity has been compromised by film and the car windscreen.'

Ballard agrees, 'It has changed the way we see the world, and the world of the imagination as well'.

The world of the imagination, I nod as I transcribe, yes this is the world that I am looking for. The description of his writing as resembling an autopsy also reminds me of auto. The car. The vehicle of the imagination.

'When I am in the driving seat,' Will Self says to Ballard, 'it's almost like I am taking dictation.'

If driving alters our view of the world, it also suggests a mode of passive activity not dissimilar to writing: for the experienced driver, the unconscious takes over the act of driving, and the consciousness is only called into play when something occurs that requires attention. Writing is also one of those acts that, if it is going well, you are barely aware of it happening at all. That is the 'taking dictation'.

I can't drive, so cars are strange to me; they are cocoons that protect you from their speed: open a window on the motorway, and velocity roars in through the crack. The interior of our vehicles, the social rituals and cultural codes surrounding these machines, conceal their lethal potential. This is the kind of consensual delusion that Will Self wants to expose by extrapolating it into an elaborate fictive hypothesis. Unfortunately, this satirical attitude to traffic also extends to his driving.

Will Self's short story 'Scale' conflates driving and writing in the form of comic 'motorway poetry'. The parallels between writer and driver converge to darker, more disturbing effect in the eponymous story of *Tough Tough Toys for Tough Tough Boys*, in which a long obsessive drive down from Orkney turns suicidal. But that dark turning lies in the future. In both stories, the driving is as obsessional as writing.

Driving is one congruence in the imaginations of Ballard and Self. Another concerns imaginative agency, or in other words, where do ideas come from?

Ballard says, 'The environments both internal and external, the outer world of everyday reality and the inner one inside my head, are constantly offering me clues to what is going on. These clues secrete obsessional material around themselves.'

I stop the tape, rewind it and play it again. Yes, he did say that.

'These clues *secrete* obsessional material around themselves.'

Secrete? That suggests some agency on behalf of the material itself.

The conversation turns around various metaphors, all of which suggest an exteriorisation of the self during the act of composition. Or to my suggestive frame of mind, the sense of an exterior agency altogether: if the writer is taking dictation, then who is giving it?

They discuss William Burroughs, another of Will Self's literary mentors. Ballard had met Burroughs on a few occasions. His essay 'Terminal Documents', published in *Ambit* in 1966, advocates Burroughs' novels, *Naked Lunch*, *Nova Express*, *Soft Machine* and *The Ticket That Exploded*; Ballard maintained that, as with Joyce, Burroughs had been overlooked due to the scatological aspects of his work – Dame Edith Sitwell protested in the *Times Literary Supplement* – *pace* Burroughs – that she did not wish to have 'her nose nailed to other people's lavatories'. Ballard claimed Burroughs as the lineal successor of James Joyce, and therefore a continuation of Modernism's literary project. Burroughs was also influenced by science fiction, citing the hip outsiders and gestalt mind of Theodore Sturgeon's

More Than Human and littering his own texts with clippings from pulp futures. If you put aside the prevailing prejudice that one belongs to high culture and the other to low culture, both Modernism and science fiction respond to anxieties and desires concerning technology.

In the interview, Ballard explains this back history of science fiction to Will Self.

'I still had hopes in those days – the Sixties had just ended, science fiction had at last begun to escape from its ghetto. A whole new raft of science fiction writers had come along who had read their Kafka, their James Joyce, they were aware of the larger world of the twentieth-century experimental novel, they were interested in Surrealism – and they could see that science fiction needed to rejoin the mainstream, even if, as I claimed then and now, it wasn't the mainstream.'

Will Self's response is admirably abrupt.

'I didn't pay any attention to that part of your thesis,' he says.

If Ballard is to be his literary mentor in the Nineties, then it cannot be as a writer of science fiction.

Ballard's advocacy of 'inner space' in the Sixties was opposed to the 'outer space' science fictions of Arthur C Clarke and Isaac Asimov, engineer stories with functional prose. Burroughs said he was writing for the 'cosmonauts of inner space' and this chimed with Ballard's ambitions for his own work. Along with Michael Moorcock, who gave Ballard his first copy of *Naked Lunch*, they touted Burroughs as a science fiction writer, even if his use of science fictional elements was in the service of irrationality. Stanislaw Lem, the author of *Solaris*, another strong influence on Will Self, saw how such irrational imagery within science fiction was a route into literary acceptance. The hope of Ballard and his cohort around the influential SF magazine *New Worlds* was that – in Lem's terms – 'by giving up the programmatic rationalism of science fiction in favor of the irrational, they try to bring about the conversion of science fiction to the creed of normal literature.'

By the early Nineties, these attempts to bring science fiction and literary fiction together had largely ceased. The genre relapses, irrevocably so as far as Ballard and Self are concerned. It would be fatal to both their ambitions to be tarred with that brush. And so the innovation of inner space is decoupled from this binary with outer space, and becomes wedded to culturally legitimate sources of inspiration: to Freud, the Surrealists, the unconscious. The cultural innovation of the Sixties is a usable past for the literary fiction writer of the Nineties, but first it must be divested of genre.

So the inner space becomes a landscape or – to use a word that crops up often in the interview – a topography. The ideas are out there as much as they are in here. 'The ideas and images have a life of their own,' says Ballard. 'They emerge through the topsoil of the mind, push forward and make their presence felt. And one then uses them as part of the larger inquiry which every novel or short story is.'

The ideas make their presence felt. I take off my headphones. My thought flits from metaphor to metaphor like a fly hopscotching up the stuck bodies of other flies. What would it be like, I wonder, to experience an idea embodied and exterior to the self, with a will of its own? Could I go out into the fields right now and watch an idea push its way up through the topsoil?

Burroughs is an example of a writer who lives in the world of the imagination in this way. Ballard explains that, in contrast to his own uncommitted affect, Burroughs 'believes everything he writes. He lives in a paranoid micro-climate of his own; the rain falls and the rain is the condensation of this paranoid climate. The rain is the material of his books.'

I am the amanuensis. I write down what writers say, and add no words of my own. My writing is entirely like taking dictation.

I decant Will's bin bags into a second-hand filing cabinet: juvenilia, receipts, bank statements, first drafts. I slide cashpoint receipts onto the spike next to the Amstrad; these receipts indicate cash withdrawals on a scale I have never seen before, in units of fifty: these are adult portions of money, and not the scrappy tenners I survived on as a student.

My wage is a hundred pounds a week, with bed and board thrown in. A decent sum.

Will writes out my list of tasks. I am to travel to London, to the A-Z shop in Chancery Lane, to buy the largest street map in stock. This map must then be mounted on a flexible screen so that we can sit inside it of an evening, reading and drinking, in his preferred mode of silence, until we are sufficiently intoxicated for bed. While in Chancery Lane I will also call in at the tobacconist to pick up a carton of filterless softpack Camels. I am to source a further twenty disks for the Amstrad (the machine is already obsolete), and speak to his friends in Orkney to arrange the transport south of a boat he bought when he was last on the island. Then to Charing Cross to buy books on firearms – small sidearms in particular – nothing too technical, with a book on wounds, also, if I can find it. From there, I am to travel to West London and scout out the estate agents, and bring back the particulars for three-bedroom properties in Acton – doer-uppers, with a big garden. He is making plans to leave Suffolk and I've only just arrived.

Then there are the domestic chores: cycling dirty laundry to the laundrette for a service wash, sweeping the fire grate, purchasing more flypaper, and cropping the opium. The desiccated poppy in the yard is an advance scout for an armada of opium poppies growing in a patch beside the copse. As it is harvest season, I am instructed to pick the opium and use my below-stairs skills to make something of it.

Late afternoon. I go out to the patch with a bin bag. There are a hundred or so heads of opium on tall stalks. Someone has already bled the poppies of their sap, their incisions a smile cut into each head. Using the bread knife, I saw the heads from their stalks and toss them into the bin bag. Then I realise that I am not alone.

'What are you doing, lad?'

He is a country man with a strong Suffolk accent. I don't have the local knowledge to be any more precise than that. Have I been caught stealing?

He walks over and I open the bag for his inspection.

'I'm going to make a tea,' I say. 'Opium tea.'

This amuses him. 'Somebody's already been at them.' He squeezes open the slit poppy head, then nods in the direction of the cottage. 'You living in one of the Franklins' places?'

'Do you know them?' I ask.

'I look after their birds,' he says. The "liner-shaped" copse is where the Franklins' pheasants roam. He is their gamekeeper. But he is also the poacher. At certain times of year, on select weeks, he is allowed to shoot Canadian geese on their migration. These birds, he explains, go into the freezer and so he never has to buy any food. He points out the combine harvester rattling along the Saxmundham road. Once the harvester sets to work on the field, he will stand on the border with his friends and wait for the rabbits to run right into their sights.

'I never go into a supermarket,' he says.

We roll our respective cigarettes.

'You got a name?'

'Matthew.'

'Col.'

'You live off the land, Col?'

'As much as a man can. I still need to work for my rent. So long as nothing happens to the Franklins' pheasants, I've got a roof over my head. You?'

'I work for the man who lives in the cottage.'

'What line of work is he in?'

'Writing.'

Col observes the social convention of being interested or impressed by the notion of the writer, but not *that* interested or impressed.

'Anything I might've read?'

Never an easy question to answer.

'*The Quantity Theory of Insanity?*' I say.

We leave it there. Col the poacher-gamekeeper walks off down Church Lane.

In the cottage, I experiment with the opium heads: boiling them up, mashing them, straining the resulting liquid and serving it with two fingers of Scotch. I name this concoction Horlicks Plus. The effects are variable and indistinct. Perhaps there is no effect at all. I decide to lie down. I am woken by the distinct rap of a knuckle on the window. I bolt upright.

The bedroom is on the second floor. No-one could knock on it without a ladder or wings.

THE LADIES OF
LLANGOLLEN

Late summer in the cottage. East across the flatland, beyond a concrete water tower, lies the small town of Leiston.

'Twinned with Sodom and Gomorrah,' I say.

Will snorts. We drive into Leiston for fish and chips. We join the line at the chippy. Will, his t-shirt revealing long tattooed arms, leans over the counter and raps a knuckle against the side of a glass jar of pickled eggs floating in cloudy vinegar. To the assembled queue, he announces, 'Never underestimate the importance of a pickled egg.'

As we cross the car park with our plastic bags of hot carbs, a line of sullen teenagers watch us closely. I bristle in anticipation of their provocations. None come. To the untrained eye, we could be mistaken for being tasty in a fight.

Martin Amis: Are you tasty in a fight?

Will Self: Against literary critics, yes.

Then speeding back to the cottage along dark country lanes with the cassette of Nirvana's 'Smells Like Teen Spirit' loud on the car stereo and hot tightly-wrapped bags of chips on my lap, to be eaten at home on proper plates. My mother's crockery has followed me to the cottage and insinuated itself into Will's possessions: it will take him many years to shake off one particular mustard-coloured Hornsea Pottery plate. My mother also off-loaded into my possession a job lot of promotional mugs for Cadbury's confectionery bar Twirl, and it is from these Twirl mugs that we drink our tea.

A journalist visits from America, and he notes my presence with some interest. Will has decided that we will serve roast chicken. He is in the kitchen, scrubbing the potatoes. The journalist holds his notebook close to his chest, signalling to us that – despite the informality of the lounge, with its second-hand sofa and the dangling strips of flypaper – we are on the record.

'We're like the Ladies of Llangollen* out here,' says Will to the journalist, plopping aside a clean potato and taking up a dirty one. The quote makes it into the piece, as he intended. Do I mind if he implies we are a gay couple to deflect questions about his broken marriage? If that's the plan, then I will go along with it.

Domesticity is strange to me. I've come from shared houses in which I consistently failed to pull my weight. Will has come hot from a family home with children in it. He turns around and checks the oven temperature. He is playing at being mother.

Will pushes his hand entirely into a plucked chicken and lifts it toward me like a large white boxing glove.

---

* The Ladies of Llangollen were two aristocratic women who eloped together to a cottage in Wales in 1778 and became 'the two most celebrated virgins in Europe'.

'Smell the bird,' he intones.

I come forward and smell the bird.

'Is it fit to eat?' he asks.

I nod at him and then toward the American journalist.

'The bird is fit to eat.'

He opens the oven door and slides in the bird.

I lay the table, cutlery and plates and three of my old mugs.

The American journalist makes a telling note in his notebook: Twirl?

After dinner, our guest leaves, and then it is just the two of us. Two strangers trying to have a quiet night in, moderating their respective needs to intoxicate themselves into sleep, as tomorrow is a working day. And Will has a strong work ethic. Every weekday morning he is at his desk between nine and ten. At his request, I have framed his colour laser printing of an artwork by Robert Williams called *In the Land of Retinal Delights*. It is a pop-psychedelic masterpiece, depicting a man in a suit sitting in an otherworld of plastic trash, his right eye massively magnified yet rendered in such detail that the tired skin beneath his eyes is scaly like crocodile skin. This image sets the tone for the working day.

After breakfast, I work on the reserve Amstrad in my bedroom, rising only to perform whatever tasks are required of me. After a productive day's work, we leave the cottage to walk beside moonlit hedgerows and across muddy fields until we come to a pub: the Chequers on the road to Aldeburgh, or the Eel's Foot Inn in Eastbridge.

In the Chequers, Will says he wants his next novel to be called Untitled. It will come in a plain cover with no page numbers and no chapter breaks and so be 'stripped of all the armature of the physical text.' What the novel consists of, line by line, we do not discuss.

After pints of Adnams with whisky chasers, we push on. Not a pub crawl but a pub stride. I feel like he is outrunning me.

The faint aura of Leiston on the horizon. Pylons straddle the blue plain. I suggest an image of sentinels marching hand-in-hand across the landscape.

'Marching pylons is a cliché,' snaps Will. 'From an advert.'

Undeterred, I try to devise more arresting images to express the intensity I feel toward the landscape: the silhouettes of trees frozen in their dance; the black plastic-wrapped pods of silage lurking on the fields and waiting to hatch.

Will snorts.

Sentences are measured out in paces, gait and voice march in unison. My cheaply-coined images interrupt Will's act of composition. I must learn to respect long silences, to hang back.

In the beer garden of the Eel's Foot Inn, batting away dusk midges, he instructs me very clearly: 'Never try to keep up with me. On drugs or drink. I've been doing this for a long time.'

He's worried that his regime may inadvertently kill me. But, at my end, it's only drink, the special cigarette and – now and again – some Horlicks Plus. He keeps the rest for himself, and that's fine.

The area is familiar to him from childhood holidays crabbing at Walberswick. He remembers his father telling him the story of how Dunwich slid into the North Sea in the eleventh century. On stormy nights, the bells of the drowned churches can still be heard ringing under the water. He talks so much about London that it comes as a surprise to discover he has strong connections to this landscape, that Suffolk is included in his memory map, and associated with his family life with his parents.

If I am to inhabit Will Self country, then I must know something of its original enclosure: his father Peter, his mother Elaine. The death of the mother is presented as the primal event in his fiction. 'The North London Book of the Dead' is the story that opens his debut collection *The Quantity Theory of Insanity: Together with Five Supporting Propositions*. The first line concerns his bereavement, which begins conventionally enough but then becomes 'bizarre and hallucinatory', a statement that stands in for the mode of his fiction in this period, the stories that unveil profound strangeness within the contemporary drab. After Mother's funeral – the story renders her as a proper noun to signal self-awareness of an obsessive bond – the narrator encounters her later in the winter of that year, 'on a drizzly, bleak Tuesday afternoon'. Mother is walking on the other side of the road, laden with bags: a handbag, a book bag, a carrier bag. The conceit of the story is that the dead do not come back to life; rather, the dead simply move to a different London suburb. This is evocative of grief, when our dead come to us in our dreams, and in that conjured world seem to have as much agency as they had in life.

The title of 'The North London Book of the Dead' parodies the Tibetan Book of the Dead, a counter-cultural touchstone of the Sixties. Its third 1957 edition includes an introduction by Carl Jung titled a 'Psychological Commentary', and here Jung writes, 'It is good that such to all intents and purposes "useless" books exist. They are meant for those "queer folk" who no longer set much store by the uses, aims and meaning of present-day "civilisation".' *Useless books* is one way of describing counter-cultural knowledge of no utility to the purposes of mainstream society. In the North London Book of the Dead, Mother – with her CND badge and her bag of books – belongs to the useless counter-cultural world of the dead, hiding from the living in plain sight.

So much for Mother. What of Father? If I am aware of Professor Peter Self, a Visiting Fellow at the Australian National

University in Canberra, it is through the satires of his academic thought peppered throughout *Quantity Theory* and subsequent stories. A recurring motif in Will Self's fiction is the British Journal of Ephemera, which scorns the marginal relevance of academic discourse. (Tellingly the motif is retired in 2011, signalling a shift in attitude both toward academia and to the intellectual achievements of Professor Peter Self). Will describes his father tasking him – as a child – to express his arguments dialectically. If the father presides over the exacting logic of professorial argument and the tedium of official discourse, then mother is the gateway to 'useless knowledge', wild and strange visions of the counter-cultural library that veers away from the ordered mainstream thought.

The parents become the oppositional terms of the dialectic – thesis and antithesis – in which the child is riven by the tensions of synthesis.

Stumbling and blundering back across the field, eyes adjusting to a deeper darkness, I am aware primarily of my inability to talk about any of this personal stuff. My upbringing was calm and stable. Like Will, I am a youngest child, with all the irresponsibility that comes from that slot in the birth order. Nothing bad has happened to me yet and so I do not know how to talk about death, pain, or any of the awkward stuff. What we share is this identification with the mother as the source and audience of our creativity, the crooked path we walk rather than follow in the footsteps of the father.

We stride across night fields in dissatisfied silence. Will is always ten yards ahead of me. I suggest a slackening of the pace.

He shouts, 'My father would think nothing of walking the five miles to Saxmundham and back,' and pushes on into the night. This is the first time I've heard Peter Self spoken of in a positive way.

In the following months, Will takes to walking the five miles to Saxmundham and back, returning to the cottage in mud-spattered jeans and an incongruously healthy spring to his step.

'The body is like a dog,' he says. 'The more you exercise it, the more exercise it demands.'

Walking aside, we do not give in to the demands of the dog. We've staked too much on the virtues of vice to change course now. This is not the time when Will comes clean. That comes much later for him. But in terms of Will Self country, I have found my bearings: vigorous walking in a straight line is the path of the father, counter-culture is the sinuous course taken by the mother.

* * *

Will is going away to Brazil on a book tour. Preparations must be made. The decks cleared. It will be my role to keep the 'whole Will Self industry' ticking over while he is away. Indeed, it is these prolonged foreign trips that were part of his reasoning for employing an amanuensis. He wanted someone at his desk while he was away. An empty desk is a source of anxiety for him. The French short story writer Guy de Maupassant wrote constantly to the point that one day he came to his study and saw himself sat right there at his desk, writing. Like Maupassant's doppelgänger, I am to keep the words moving, to turn over the soil of Will Self Country so that it does not dry up.

Will goes through my tasks: who I am to call and request a deadline extension from, and the people I am to chase. Bruce Wagner still hasn't called. The author of *Force Majeure* and 'Wild Palms' is being lined up to adapt *My Idea of Fun* for the cinema. Oliver Stone will direct. I am to call his agent but I must work on my politeness.

There have been complaints about my phone manner.

For example: a woman calls. It's Victoria. 'No, it isn't,' explains the voice at the other end of the line, 'Victoria is Will's mistress. This is his wife, Kate.' I apologise, and explain that because I am Liverpudlian, all posh women sound the same to me. She accepts my apology, or tactfully ignores it.

There is no animosity between Kate and Victoria, no sense that their relationships with Will had overlapped. Still, the point stands: I must improve my phone manner. But not everyone who calls has a good phone manner. Another writer, for example, will leave a long message explaining that he has AIDS and is dying. Will is quite shaken by this. A week later, the writer will leave another message on the answering machine which I summarise thusly: '[X] called. Re: AIDS. Doesn't really have it. Apologies.'

Preparations take place across a rational day of business, the making and taking of long phone calls with commissioning editors, writers, agents and publishers. Calls from Marti Blumenthal, Will Blythe and Carlo Gebler, Jane Thomas from *Observer* magazine and Julie from Bloomsbury. I remind Will that Tim Adams has or wants the details on St Kilda, that Rory-Knight Bruce wants to talk about hop-picking. That he really should call Tim Adams, it seems urgent.

I lurk at the back of the office, beside the Italian typewriters in their dust covers, waiting to come forward with hot tea in a Twirl mug. His long desk is surrounded by Post-it notes: I track the appearance of new notes, such as the one that reads 'axe-headed turd'. (This will later become the hatchet-headed turd found in a nappy in the novel *Great Apes*). The rhythms of the study: the whirring clunk of the Amstrad word processor, the blinking monochrome cursor of the VDU, the pebble of hashish beside the Anglepoise lamp, the tarry dog-ends in the

Q-shaped metallic ashtray purloined from Quaglinos. I put the tea down on the desk, next to a pile of alternative magazines from all over the world; magazines like the *Nose* from San Francisco, *Hermenaut* coming out of Boston, the RE:SEARCH volume on Ballard sourced for the interview, and a couple of copies of the *Idler*, one with Homer Simpson on the cover and one with Kurt Cobain, beside the line 'Blown away', a reference to the rock star's suicide by shotgun.

Before he flies to Brazil, Will has to leave for Manchester. Every two weeks he appears on Mark and Lard's Radio 5 show and introduces a counter-cultural text or cult book to their audience: *Steppenwolf* by Herman Hesse, Céline's *Journey to the End of the Night*, *The Story of O*, *Junky* by William Burroughs, Pynchon's *The Crying of Lot 49*, and Kerouac's *On the Road* – that restless, wandering novel. He borrows my copy, and will later return it to me with his Post-it notes still inside: one reads 'Hipster, Cassidy, Junky, Gins. Electric Kool Aid. Def of "BEAT"', another 'Influence of novel – 60s MYSTICISM. DHARMA BUMS.'

***

No sooner has a cab arrived to take Will away than the doorbell rings again.

It's my driving instructor, Mike: tidy moustache, beige sports jacket, jeans, black loafers. Will is adamant that I learn to drive. It will be helpful for running messages and will reduce the likelihood of him wiping us out with rash overtaking on a Sunday afternoon.

The next thing I know I'm driving a bloody car.

We drive up the high-hedged lane, winding across the flatlands toward Aldeburgh. In the town, I get stuck on a hill start on a tight corner. Unlike Will, the driving instructor cannot simply leave the room when I'm talking. With Mike, I take the opportunity to blather.

'I'm still too much in love with metaphor to be a good driver,' I explain to Mike. I try to restart the car but I haven't engaged the handbrake. I over-rev the engine to stop the car's backwards roll, and then remember the handbrake, and engage it just as the clutch hits biting point, stalling the car again.

'You see, the car is a mechanical device so I must operate its pedals and levers in sequence.'

Looking down, I attempt to operate the pedals and levers in sequence.

'If I try to reach ahead in the sequence, say, by pulling the handbrake before I've come to a stop, then things go wrong.'

I rev so hard on biting point that the bonnet of the car rides up. In the rear-view mirror, hand gestures in the windscreen of the car behind.

'Now I release the brake…' we drive off, 'and it's all one thing after another with driving. Mirror. Signal. Manoeuvre. There's no room for improvisation. Whereas metaphors are created by the collision of one concept into another – if I say that truth is light, for example, then one thing – the abstract concept of truth – is transformed into a visual image of bright white light. Clarity. Clarity is very important, Mike.'

'Could you take the next left?'

'I missed it. I'll get around to left in a minute.'

We trundle down a lane running parallel to the seafront, passing yellow and blue cottages, fisherman's huts and B&Bs. There are deckchairs on the terraces, gazing out at the enormity of sea and sky. I find a left turn, and notice that there are opium poppies in the lawns of the pink cottages of Crabbe Street, named after the romantic poet George Crabbe. He was a small-time Aldeburgh surgeon then clergyman whose verse attracted praise from Byron and Samuel Johnson. I decide to show off my local and literary knowledge, airing one of my proto-Selfian riffs, speaking with my master's voice.

'Crabbe's first major work was about drink,' I discourse to Mike. '"Inebriety", as in inebriation. Crabbe describes "the muddy ecstasies of beer", which is a nice line. Not that poets can drive. Or if they can, their poetry is rarely worth the trouble, as Martin Amis says. Wait, is this street one-way?'

It is. I must perform a three-point turn.

I enjoy a captive audience because Will doesn't do small-talk. We eat most of our dinners in silence while he snorts his way through the *New Yorker*, or the New Umlaut as he christens it, after the magazine's fussy habit of putting a diuresis on consecutive 'e's: as in, reënactment. In the cottage, I have to choose my words carefully, and avoid swingeing generalisations.

Not so with my driving instructor.

I don't give a shit what I say to Mike.

Three-point turn completed, the car hops forward as I resume my struggle with the clutch. At no point do I stop talking.

I say to Mike, 'Poetry is compacted, collided language. That's why poets are terrible drivers. Whereas prose is just one bloody thing after another, and so prose writers can drive for three hundred, four hundred miles without a break.'

We brake suddenly and it's not my doing. I look accusingly at Mike. He has his own set of pedals.

'Red light,' he says, pointing at the crossing.

'I know.'

'Were you going to stop?'

'Of course. Just because I'm talking doesn't mean that I'm not concentrating.'

I drive back toward Leiston. The roads are too flat and empty to be an effective course of instruction. I decide to overtake some youths in a hatchback to demonstrate that just because I am a learner driver, I am not to be trifled with.

'What are you doing?' yelps Mike.

'I don't want to be obvious,' I reply, accelerating fiercely. I don't want to be generic. We must be more innovative in our forms. Isn't this how Will drives, too? The engine revs and whirs at my command and then the car lists out into the right-hand lane. In the hatchback, a vague sense of youths making obscene gestures.

'I'm trying to get my unconscious to do more of the hard work,' I explain to Mike as I pull the car back in again.

'You're going too fast,' says Mike.

'I've proved my point.'

I slow down. Affronted, the hatchback overtakes me in turn.

Mike wants me to concentrate more. He doesn't understand how attentiveness works. The first time Mike took me to a roundabout, it seemed like the intricate clockwork workings of a giant watch. It was too much for me to apprehend consciously. But my unconscious mind can handle the complexity. Talking helps. Talking moves the responsibility for driving down from my conscious mind into to my unconscious. Only when I can drive without *thinking* – automatically, as if taking dictation – will I truly be a driver.

With some relief, Mike drops me off at the cottage. The front door is open but nobody is home. In the office, on the keyboard of the Amstrad, there is a brace of dead ducks, two silvery-green mallards with limp necks.

Has Will returned early from Manchester? No. Someone else has been here.

I don't want to touch the dead birds, not with my fingers.

Should I put the ducks in the fridge? Or are they here for

another reason? That is, do the ducks belong to the category of food or to the category of communication? Likely both. The ducks are a message and that is why they have been placed over the keyboard. I wish my driving instructor was still with me, so we could discuss it. I'm not very good at figuring out the bloody obvious.

I leave the ducks in situ, take out my bicycle and ride to the ruins of Leiston Abbey for further rumination, then onto the cinema for an early evening screening of *Casablanca*. When Bogart lights another cigarette, I'm indignant to discover that smoking is not permitted in the auditorium even though I constitute the entire audience. How am I expected to watch a film in which everyone smokes without smoking myself? Society is losing its way.

I emerge from *Casablanca*. It's dark and I don't have any lights for my bike. I navigate along the dark lanes by the reflection of the moon wavering in the mudguard. The ride is spooky, the silence so distracting I almost come off at the bend where the verge conceals a deep stagnant pond. I freewheel down a tunnel cored through the overgrown valley, can't see where the road ends, can't see where I'm going, trusting entirely to my memory of the humps and dips of the tarmac.

The cottage is empty. The ducks are still on the keyboard. Food or communication? A message from whom? To whom? From Will to me? Are we two ducks, sprawled out on our keyboards?

Spooked, I load the air rifle with a pellet and go from room to room in the manner of a SWAT agent. Finding no-one, I return to the study.

I'm feeling the *vibe*, I'm cockshrunk and dithery and I haven't even checked the shed yet. The axe is in there. Better an axe than an air rifle. I go out into the garden. The night sky is clear and the star field is busy overhead. If I go into the shed, I will be giving in to the vibe, taking instruction from fear, and that will only lead to more fear. I defy the vibe. I turn my back on the shed and piss into the broken greenhouse, urine spattering blackly upon the stinging nettles. Pissing outside is becoming a habit. An animalistic urge to mark territory.

I don't want to go back into the house. Not yet. A thorough inspection of the grounds is required. Only then will I be satisfied that I am not afraid.

I walk the moonlit muddy path that borders the wheat field, then past the savaged opium patch. I find something strange nailed to a tree: I step aside so the moonlight can illuminate it. It is a box, containing the wing-bones of a raven and other meaty bits and bobs strung together by wire. Bait. Or warning. Some kind of magical work, I think. An incantation in flesh, iron and wood.

In the ditch, at my feet, I see a dead rabbit, its flesh withered so that its lip has a cynical curl. In its hollow ocular orbit, a bright black-and-red spotted ladybird swivels this way and that, mimicking the missing eye. It reminds me of Robert Williams' illustration, *In the Land of Retinal Delights*, that suited man with a single giant eye roaming a strange landscape, his iris riddled with reflections of the multi-coloured artificial abstract trash of his surroundings.

I rock on my haunches and prod the dead rabbit with a stick so that the ladybird unfurls its wings. The eye takes flight. I am alone again.

QUITE UNNECESSARY

On quiet nights alone, I submerge myself in Will Self's library. The night breeze riffles the flypaper; these yellow strips, the gum dry and dusty, augur autumn. I lie on a second-hand sofa, a garish thing and too short for a tall man to recline upon with any languor. It is entirely not the chaise longue we require.

The living room is a cold and uncomfortable place. The fire is in the study but I can't relax there because it is Will's place. My stereo, my only significant possession, is here; on Will's instruction, I've bought CDs of Vaughan Williams and Thomas Tallis but he has ordained that we must not read and listen to music at the same time. We must concentrate on one or the other, else we become inattentive. Tolstoy, in his essay on Maupassant, cited the quality of attentiveness as indispensable for good writing. Saul Bellow, reflecting on this, noted that 'by attending closely, the writer was to breed attentiveness in his readers, replacing the world with *his* world.' If life in the cottage is to be designed entirely around the requirements of the writer, then our routines must train this faculty of heightened noticing, and through the conviction of our attentiveness persuade others of our fictions.

The wind tests the loose window like an opportunistic thief. I go out into the garden to urinate. A bank of shadowed nettles clamour for my piss, and I do not disappoint them. It feels right to piss in the corner of the garden, to briefly commingle myself and nature.

Returning to the sofa, I take up Baudelaire's *Les Fleurs du Mal.* I make a note of Baudelaire's opening line: 'I have not forgotten our white cottage'.

> *Je n'ai pas oublié, voisine de la ville,*
> *Notre blanche maison, petite mais tranquille.*

The indolent recollection of 'I have not forgotten' accords with my reclined position. Smoke wisps and whirls under the bare light bulb. The past is elusive and scant. Forgetting protects us from it, and keeps us moving forward. The merciful absences of forgetting permit abstraction, and therefore fiction.

The next morning, on my way downstairs, I notice something new. Not the dead bee on the windowsill, which has been there for so long its corpse is clad in a parka of dust, rather, Sellotaped next to it, there is a two-inch square sign memorialising the life of the bee in the style of the National Trust. The sign was the last thing Will wrote before he left for Rio.

Downstairs, Glynnis the cleaner helps herself to tea. She doesn't know what to do about the bee, now that Will's tiny sign has drawn our attention to it. Does the sign mean what it says about the need to preserve the bee as part of our heritage? Will and I don't run a fastidious house but we are making an effort. After my first attempt to wash-up, Will instructed me 'on the importance of clean work surfaces', gesturing at me with the special cigarette pinched between the yellow fingers of a pair of Marigold gloves. When it came to meeting his standards, I didn't need asking twice. Although I did need asking. If only he'd told me that duvet covers do not wash themselves then I would have been spared the embarrassment, when he had guests over, and I was away, of them discovering that – in Will's words – 'your duvet is about eighty per cent sperm'.

The morning light comes in through the grimy kitchen window. Glynnis drinks her tea, makes another, then wafts the hoover around. The postman delivers padded envelopes containing cassette tapes from a friend of mine called Nelson, who works in a pub. I have asked him to record conversations at the bar. My plan is that I will transcribe these tapes just as I transcribed the conversation between Will Self and JG Ballard. I have a vague plan for a story about a collector of such tapes called William Mooch. Mooch can source, for the right price, a recording of any conversation a client requests; the pillow talk of the rich and powerful, the itemised guilt of the confession booth, and all the things they say about you behind your back. The Dictaphone is an instrument that allows the hoarding of intimate ephemera, much like my duvet.

I ride out to the sea to record the conversation of the waves as they break upon the shore. Will suggested that, in his absence, I try to bring objects out of my dreams into the real world, a further exercise in attentiveness. To this end, I follow the experiments of the Surrealists. I place tin trays either side of the bed, then try falling asleep with handfuls of cutlery. The moment I lose consciousness, I let go of the cutlery, it crashes against the tray, waking me instantly from the hypnagogic state, the most fecund condition of dreaming, a running flush of unexpectedly conjoined words and inexpressible hybrids, which I quickly write down.

The cutlery crashes. I have a vision of myself standing in front of the white dome of Sizewell B holding a frying pan, the shape of a crescent moon cut into its metal base. This curved slice is filled with radioactive luminosity.

Dutifully, I ride into Leiston and ask an ironmonger to cut the necessary shape out of my frying pan, explaining that I wish to re-enact my vision on the beach and so bring the dream object into the physical realm. The ironmonger chases me from his yard.

Further surrealistic experimentation takes place in my bedroom. I snip words from the gardening pages of the *Daily Telegraph* and mix them in a bag with words cut from the book review pages. Words taken at random from the bag arrange themselves into mystical pointers indicating occulted truths: the secrets of the book review pages are revealed in the emerging sentence, 'Disputatious public mouths with the agenda of a damaging inquisition.' Mixing a pinch of the gardening column with a handful of words from a review of the philosophy primer *Sophie's World* indicates that 'rationality is a material that rats inform us of with their humane remarks'. By making myself attentive, I will discover the hidden connections between things. To this end, there must be intensity at all times. In Will's empty bedroom, there is a tiny jar of amyl nitrate on the bedside table and a quart of whisky under the bed.

Will calls.

'How's Brazil?' I ask.

'It's like the Klingon Empire,' he hisses and laughs. 'The door opened and someone threw a *gunnysack* of cocaine into the hotel room. I haven't been out much.'

'The book festival?'

He recounts a series of scrapes, scandals, feuds. 'I've caused an international incident!' Who knew book festivals could be so combative? He is interrupted by something going on outside.

'They're shooting!' he shouts. 'They're shooting!'

He holds the phone outside the window so that I can hear the gunfire. I can't hear any gunfire.

I tell him the car repairs are going to come to eight hundred and fifty quid. The news does not go down well, nor does it go down badly. It does not go down *at all*; it is a too-prosaic reminder of home when he is so juiced among the Klingons. What was it Winnicott said? I came to it while transcribing the conversation between Will Self and the writer-psychoanalyst Adam Phillips. The artist is the exemplary man by virtue of his 'non-compliance'. Guilt, in which memory forces you to attend over and again to wrongdoing, can – Phillips writes – be obviated or forestalled by the artist 'in order to follow his purpose ruthlessly.' This is my role in the life of Will Self: I am here to aid his non-compliance because non-compliance is how we make ourselves attentive to the true social relations that control us, and our psychological internalisation of these convenient truths. I must not – in any way – contribute to his sense of guilt or obligation; even at twenty-two years old, I understand that completely. In my notebook, I quote Antonin Artaud: 'you are quite unnecessary, young man'.

Over the phone, I take further instruction from Will. He thinks it's time I cleared away the flypaper. It can't be healthy, can it? Then he is interrupted by someone joining him in the hotel room. At that same moment, a van pulls up outside the cottage, and so the phone call ends in mutual interruption. Two burly men get out of the van and knock at the door. Bailiffs! How many times, as a licence-dodging, fare-evading student have I rehearsed this moment? I answer the door cautiously. But the bailiffs are looking for somebody else, a previous tenant. I am polite but uninformative.

The transit pulls away and then Col the gamekeeper emerges from out of the copse.

'Friends of yours?' he asks.

'Bailiffs,' I explain. 'Looking for somebody else this time.'

'The man who lived here before you?'

'Did you know him?'

Col shakes his head, cleans the dried mud from his thick fingertips. Col has been in the copse, checking on the pheasants, counting them. Shooting season is in just over a month. It's very important the shooting parties have the requisite number of birds. Until October, the pheasants are indulged like so many feathered princes.

In a couple of days, he says, he'll be able to shoot the Canadian geese over by the reserve and put a couple in his freezer for winter.

That reminds me. 'I found two dead ducks on our keyboard, in the office. Did you leave them there?'

Col denies all knowledge of the mallards. I took the ducks into town to be plucked and cleaned by the butcher. They were on the turn.

I have more questions for Col.

'I went out walking the other night, and found, in the copse, a shelter made out of a couple of hay bales and some corrugated iron. There was a box nailed to a tree and it contained a raven's wing strung with wire. Is that yours?'

Col shuffles uneasily.

I press the point. 'Is the raven's wing to scare off other birds, to keep them from the winter wheat?'

He looks past me, into the office of the cottage, to see if anyone else is at home. He is unreadable for so many reasons: he is weathered by the land and I am raw with education. He is old, I am too young to know how to read the shadows and lines of faces. I can't seem to find the words to put us at our mutual ease. At university, the students were at pains to emphasise their commonality, and to conceal differences in privilege. By comparison, older men like Col are disinterested in consensus or, in Will's case, actively opposed to it. Will teaches me a word for it: 'unbiddable', which appears in the two-volume edition of the OED stacked in pride of place on the mantelpiece but not my large Collins dictionary. I lose all respect for the Collins dictionary.

If words fall out of common usage, they are weeded out from dictionaries. So Will Self's deployment of lexical curiosities – *long words* – sustains the diversity of possible thought. The more precise the word, the more exact the thought; it is a social good. Wrangling long words into your style puts more signal into it, and scrubs out the noise. The problem is that most readers need the noise. Prose can be too dense. It needs to be watered down. On the other hand, it should not be chummy. Will teaches me the term of 'phatic speech'. The phatic parts of speech are the bits that carry minimal content but which seek to establish a social bond: in his stories, phatic is often rendered in a compound slur: as in, 'whassat?' 'thassit', or the covert Semitic accusation of 'Whadjewsay'? I'm partial to 'knowarramean' because it summaries the coercive property of the phatic, it's the kind of speech that puts its hand on your shoulder and calls you 'mate' or 'darling'. Will Self's style resists coercion nor does it seek, in turn, to coerce. His vocabulary expands my mind, it gives me words for thoughts that were previously inchoate.

Having used up my daily allocation of conversation with Col, I return to the office. All day, I sit in Will Self's chair, at Will Self's computer, answering mail, paying bills, writing letters and bits of fiction, then at night, I lie on the sofa under the flies with a different book from Will Self's library. I can't bring myself to take the flypaper down. Not yet.

I read Balzac's *Eugénie Grandet*. The provincial thoughts of young Eugénie are conflated with the lie of the land, her country cottage similar to ours in being 'a dismal, hedged-in prospect, yet not wholly devoid of those mysterious beauties which belong to solitary or uncultivated nature.' In pathetic fallacy, the landscape is contiguous with a frame of mind or – to quote Amiel – 'a state of the soul, and whoever knows how to read both is astonished to find likenesses across every detail.' I am susceptible to this way of thinking, in which the boundaries of the self are porous, and an indecent quantity of our emotion spills out into nature. It is a symptom of my sickly innocence.

I return to the garden to urinate. The fields are adrift and purposeless, whereas the pylons are striding off into the future, migrating, leaving me behind. The feeling is a commingling of loneliness and frustrated ambition; how can I get on in life if I never interact with other people?

When I was a security guard in Liverpool, I once had to look after a theatre. In the lobby, various young people of my age were gathered, well-to-do aspirant members of the rarer-spotted Liverpudlian bourgeoisie, players in a young orchestra and singers in a choir, on their way to a foreign engagement. They did not give me a second glance, in my navy uniform and peaked cap. Of course they didn't. I could barely control my thwarted egotism, on the wrong side of the barrier, with my clipboard and walkie-talkie. The word is 'chippy'. Will taught me that also. 'Don't be too chippy. People don't like it.' 'Chippy' is included in the Collins but it does not include this particular usage under its definitions, which would be something like 'Chippy *adj*. Display of working-class credentials to undermine unspoken middle-class consensus'. Being chippy is like being *gauche* (another new word for me) – a tedious leftward drift. He also teaches me the correct pronunciation of *hyperbole* (hi-per-bo-lee) and the meaning of *shibboleth*, the word that, in its pronunciation, acts as a test or stumbling block to entering a particular class. A wider vocabulary permits social mobility, upward or downward. We must master the demotic and the high style, and be able to ventriloquise the careful self-erasure of civil servant mandarin as smoothly as the argot of the crack dealer. Will calls dealers 'the men with writing on their trousers', encountered in the shadowed concrete tiers of underground car parks. The image defamiliarises the drug dealer by ignoring the salient details of the drugs and the dealing; instead, by focusing upon the branding written on tracksuit bottoms, seeing it as just more writing, (as if, in the author's obsession, the world is divided primarily into different forms of writing) we imbibe a sensibility that steps back from consensual reality to sport an ironic authorial unworldliness.

I ride to Aldeburgh in the hope of casual conversation, but the hotel in which I take tea is otherwise deserted. The bell rings for service, twice, thrice. This, I decide, will be the last thing I ever hear, when I lie dying on some thickly carpeted hallway at the end of a long indignity in servitude, a bell ringing again and again for service, and finally going unanswered by me.

I ride back to the cottage, getting home at dusk. The nights are growing cold. I lock up my bike in the shed, heft the clean axe over my shoulder, and walk the rutted path toward the liner-shaped copse. The darkening fields are flat and open. I will gather wood from the heart of the copse, make a fire, feel powerful again. Thick branches obstruct me like the rusted spindles of a dead machine run aground in the mulch. I push through to a tight little glade where the air is hot and close. I roll up my sleeves, locate a likely-looking branch and swing the axe down upon it. My elbows judder with the blow but it merely flakes the bark. Now that I'm chopping wood, I realise I don't know how to chop wood. But how hard can it be? Again I swing the axe and bring it down hard, missing the slice of the previous stroke and lightly marring the damp branch. The axe is keen, I am big and strong. Why can't I even chop a branch in two? Why can't I even do *that*? Sweat on my back, breathing heavily, I feel the frustration as an urgent fight-or-flight in my coccyx, the instinct to haul ass. I must swing harder, bring down my full strength upon the branch. From over my shoulder, the blade speeds downward and scuffs the branch, inverting it suddenly so that the heavy muddy end rears up and strikes me hard on the forehead.

Pain and blood and shock.

The branch, having bounced up in the air, falls slowly to earth.

So do I.

So does the axe.

Let us while away the time while I am unconscious by going over the various facts my younger self is ignorant of: that some woods are harder than others, that a branch should be secured or wedged before attempting to chop it, not that such a wet branch would burn anyway. A small saw is much better for this kind of work than an axe, which is more suited to halving heavy dry logs.

Coming to, I stagger ignorantly around the glade, axe head trailing through the undergrowth. The pain intensifies as the shock subsides. I am furious that I cannot wind back time and undo my stupidity, my needless stupidity. I can't even chop a branch. I've been educated to the level at which I can just about apprehend the inadequacy of my education. How am I supposed to make something of myself in this world when I am ignorant of its shibboleths?

I'm going to fail, aren't I? I'm going to fucking *fail*.

And then the laughter begins. A pheasant, plump and brazen, runs laughing across my path. Haw-haw-haw, it can't contain itself. Laughter is contagious. Other pheasants emerge from the bushes, roaring with amusement at my gaucheness, my provincial ways, my callow misapprehensions concerning the true nature of British society and my marginal position within it.

'What's wrong with you?' I hiss at the pheasants. 'Why are you laughing at me?'

I wheel around and confront one pheasant in particular. Its beak open, amber tongue clucking. I heft the axe up and loom over the bird, blood striping my forehead and sticky in my eyebrows.

'Why don't you run?'

The bird cocks its head contemptuously at my impotent threat.

'Don't I look like a fucking predator to you?'

Clearly not. The pheasant is indifferent. It turns its back on me. So my rage floods out from the base of the coccyx and washes me away, rage that flows not only from myself as I am but from the thwarted man I will become. The head of the axe crushes the bird in two, and the semi-severed parts of the bird turn and scratch in the deep soil. I bring the axe head up for a killing blow and the pheasant comes with it, and hangs briefly from the blade then falls to earth. It turns against itself in attempting to flee. The next blow is easy. The bird's head disappears into the dark loamy soil. The laughter is choked off.

I am the student with the hatchet. Raskolnikov. I take out the bin bag in my belt, which I brought with me for the chopped wood. I place my hands inside the bag so that it forms a pair of black plastic gloves and then, with face averted, gather up the warm entangled pieces of pheasant.

* * *

Sometimes I talk to people on the phone. My mother Sylvia calls. She doesn't like to call in case she interrupts *something*. Once my mum called to ask me for help with her word processor but I was out so she asked Will if he could provide her with IT support. To his credit, he did.

'We're thinking of visiting you,' she says. 'Because you're on your own.' Her voice sounds high and Scouse.

Mine is low and mannered.

'Well, mother, if that is what you feel you must do.'

'We haven't seen you for such a long time.'

'Liverpool is so far away. And I have a job now. I have to keep the whole Will Self industry ticking over. That is my purview.'

My voice is as unfamiliar to me as the recordings on my Dictaphone. When did I start to drawl in this fashion? When did I adopt such arch, tired formality? I must speak normally. But what do I normally sound like?

Sylvia says, 'There is a Caravan Club site not far from you.'

'Of course. The caravan.' I cannot say the word 'caravan' in my new voice without taking sardonic pleasure in its mediocre repetition of a vowel: ca-ra-van.

'You sound different. Have you got a cold?'

'Yes.' No.

'Is it cold in Suffolk? Has the weather turned where you are?'

The weather. Food. News – which is how my mother refers to my reports concerning my quest to become a writer. Any news, she will ask hopefully. These are the sanctioned categories of our discourse.

'The weather is fine.'

'Any news?'

'I've been chopping wood.'

'I hope you're being careful.'

'A branch popped up when I hit it and struck me on the head.'
She gasps.

'I'm fine though.'

'Do you need stitches?'

'How would I know if I need stitches?'

'Is it a wide cut? Have you cleaned it with TCP?'

'No, no. It's fine. I got off lightly, considering.'

'Considering what?'

'You should see the other guy,' I say.

'We always keep a first-aid kit in the car. You need a medicine cabinet in that cottage of yours.'

'Medicine,' I say the word quietly, inquiring as to the possibilities of its vowels. Med-di-cine. Included on the list of chores Will left for me was the purchase of two bottles of kaolin and morphine. The pharmacist was suspicious that I wanted two bottles. He looked me up and down. I had taken the precaution of wearing a t-shirt and a healthy smile so that he could see that my arms were free of tracks, scarring and other junkie marks. In Will Self's short story 'Scale', the protagonist produces a smokable narcotic paste from kaolin and morphine, and then takes to injecting it into his veins so that the chalky deposits from the kaolin build up into roadways raised upon the surface of the flesh.

My parents will pop by the cottage as they are in the area anyway, investigating another branch of the family tree. Since my father retired from the police force, giving up the job not long after his fiftieth birthday, he has been researching the family tree. He still takes the odd job as a freelance detective, mainly insurance fraud, filming supposedly bed-bound claimants climbing up tall ladders to repair roofs or barrow cement around the yard. He has no interest in the more conventional private detective work: cheating spouses and suchlike. He doesn't want to get involved with people, and who can blame him? *People.* He prefers staking-out some minor fraudster, following them at a discreet distance as they go about their day, then handing the tapes over to the insurance company to do what they will – this is how he likes it. Clean and discreet. The eavesdropping and confessions recorded on my Dictaphone are whimsical reflections of my father's detached surveillance of people.

When Eddie is not tailing people on foot and by car then he is travelling with my mother Sylvia in the caravan around the country, chasing up leads on the ultimate cold case: who is he? We are the Humphreys family but the surname of his mother and his father was De Abaitua. This discrepancy is a gap indicating the removal of a secret.

The only person I had spoken to about this secret was my maternal grandmother, Florence. 'People did a lot strange things in the war,' was how Florence put it. 'Did a lot of things they wouldn't have dared to do in ordinary times.'

Frank and Ethel De Abaitua split up in the war. Eddie was born in 1943, conceived before the marital split. Frank De Abaitua thought his son had been spirited away to work on the cotton mills in East Lancashire but he was living much closer to Liverpool, in Litherland, where he was raised by his grandmother with the married surname of Humphreys. Frank and Ethel already had two girls. Ethel, knowing how much her estranged husband wanted a son, decided to conceal Eddie's existence from Frank, and so punish him for leaving her for another woman. To this end, Ethel bribed the registrar with bottles of whisky to change the name on Eddie's birth certificate. Instead of De Abaitua, baby Eddie was to be called Morton, the name of the family who were going to adopt him. But then his grandmother intervened and she took Eddie in. Her married name was Humphreys, and it was to love and honour her that Eddie took that name.

My father actually has a second birth certificate where his name is recorded as Arthur Edward De Abaitua. It only turned up recently, thanks to the digitisation of the archives. As a young man he reversed the order of his first names, bringing Edward to the fore. This renaming marked the transition from the person he was, a self he had no control over, to the man he aspired to be.

At the age of twenty-two, I don't know much about my father's past, partly because I am young and self-obsessed, but mostly because Eddie has never really spoken about it. In fact, through my entire upbringing, there hasn't been much opportunity for us to talk. Now and again, he did want to talk to me but what was there to say? He had not been parented himself – what were fathers supposed to do with youngest sons, the accidental third (my superfluity is playfully admitted in my name, Matthew, chosen by my mother because it means gift from God). At home, he didn't talk about *the job*, not in front of the children, and Eddie and Sylvia never talked politics; my mother had been raised a staunch socialist by her gas-fitter father whereas Eddie, barely raised at all, had seized upon the self-created individualism of Margaret Thatcher. Would we talk about school or education? He never asked about that either, perhaps out of insecurity. Eddie left education without much by the way of qualifications. All I knew about his schooling was that his classmates – who called him 'Black Ned' for his silent brooding presence – set fire to the classroom while they were all still in it. He walked away from their crime, kept on walking out of childhood and directly into the police force and manhood. What else might we have spoken about? Women? He was married at twenty-one. Culture? Fiction bored him. He could just about sit through an episode of *The Sweeney*, and even then, as a one-time member of a flying squad himself, he was constantly taking exception to inaccuracies in their methods. Football. Yes, we talked about football. On our knees together, we played Subbuteo and he commentated on the action. He loved to play strategy games: he played a war board game called Campaign with my older brother, and taught us cribbage on long camping holidays in France. He had a little cribbage board with coloured pegs. All the policemen had one, to while away the hours on long stake-outs.

It didn't matter if Eddie came home at six o'clock or midnight, his dinner was always just about to go on the table. If I had a time machine, I would travel back to teatime. Six o'clock or thereabouts, waiting for my father to come home on any given weekday so that we can all eat. And what's for tea, Mum? A lamb chop or pork chop, boiled potatoes and peas. Fish on a Thursday, *finny-addy* (yellow-dyed haddock, fried until the flesh is tight, and served with butter) or cod with parsley sauce. Scouse in the pressure cooker, reproducing the surface conditions of Venus in an attempt to tenderise the meat. At the end of the month, in the week before payday, mince and onions and mash. For afters, pineapple chunks or pear halves served with the juice from the tin and a drizzle of evaporated milk. Perhaps a glacé cherry to remind us that we are going up in the world.

Sylvia and Eddie married young, my mother in her late teens. The single photograph of their wedding shows two gawky kids cutting a cake. Eddie's face is tight and malnourished – unmothered, frankly. That was the pact Sylvia and Eddie made with one another: he would go out and provide and she would focus on the domestic realm, always be there for the children when they came home, bake and sew and budget to make ends meet with his pay. This was the life they created for themselves.

The early Sixties was a period of social mobility for the

working class. Liverpool was being rebuilt, its people reinvented. Eddie and Sylvia bought a plot for a house on Whinney Brook Farm in Maghull, an unremarkable village on the flat Lancashire plains, nine miles out from the city, a village in the process of becoming a suburb: fields of black soil laid to cabbages and potatoes were paved over with crescents, closes and avenues, fresh vegetable odours lingering over the new tarmac and concrete.

Sylvia, pregnant, took the bus from Bootle to watch her house being built, her belly swelling with her first child (not me!). I imagine gestation running in time lapse alongside the raising of the thin brick walls, my brother kicking and turning in amniotic fluid, growing fingernails and teeth as glazers fit windows and builders bring up the cement for the path, and no sooner have the sticky rolls of tarmac dried upon new roads than the moving van arrives, with its back doors open, and a baby is brought out into the dream. Eddie, Sylvia and baby have their first Sunday lunch as a family, my father at the head of the table and served first, too, a whole chicken leg and a slice of breast. At supper time on a Sunday (dinner was the midday meal, tea the evening meal, supper served sometime between nine and eleven, depending on the movements of the men), Sylvia would always bring out the chicken carcass for Eddie, sat in the prime armchair in his dressing gown, to pick clean.

Eddie retired as soon as he could to honour his side of the bargain. After all those years of making do, of not helping around the home, this would be their time together. The children got on with their lives, and husband and wife travelled the world by caravan and cruise ship.

Eddie and Sylvia collect me from the cottage. We drive to the caravan for a barbecue and a beer. Later, my older brother Andrew will tell me that, at this stage of my life, he and my father had 'written me off'. Because I had failed to get onto a clear career path with a large organisation, I had effectively crippled my chances of getting on before I had even begun. Certainly, I never consult with my parents concerning any of my plans, including living and working with Will Self. The rightness or wrongness of my actions is never raised. I choose a path and it is one outside of their experience and I am left to walk it, exercising the prerogative of the youngest son.

Over the course of the evening, my lugubrious drawl morphs back into my former Scouse voice. My father and I get drunk and talk significantly for the first time. Something is on his mind. He pours us both two fingers of brandy.

'I've traced the family tree back a couple of hundred years now,' says Eddie. 'The De Abaituas came over to Liverpool from the Basque country.'

My father looked up his old man a few times over the course of the job. He never tried to contact him. But, now he has retired, he has been to see Frank De Abaitua. Tracing his father's whereabouts was pretty much the first thing he did on leaving the force. He approached the family first by letter, and then when they assented to meet him, he went over to the house. Turned out that Frank De Abaitua and his family lived not far from us in Maghull.

I would only meet Frank once. Frank De Abaitua had been a merchant seaman, and had jumped ship in New York. He'd been arrested in South America after a mass bar brawl, and forced to wash the police horses by way of punishment. Not that he was a fighter. He was half my size. Back in Liverpool, he ran a chippy in Fazakerley and raised a daughter with his new wife. In any marriage, one family takes precedence over the other: throughout my childhood, my mother's large family, the Batemans, the brothers and sisters from the bombed-out terraces of Bootle, were dominant. As Eddie spoke about his father, I could see a twinkle of reservation in my mother's face toward these arrivistes, these De Abaituas. She indulged my father his enthusiasm, in the same way she would roll her eyes whenever my father adopted new words and pronunciation from new friends. Being raised without a father must have made him susceptible to influence, unsure of how to make his way in the world – two problems that the police solved. They provided moral guidance and career structure. My father did very well in the police. He was ambitious, despite the burnt husk of his education; he passed the sergeant's exam first time, the inspector's exam at the second attempt, and was never distracted from the law. The police gave him a strong sense of how to behave in the world. Of how to be good. The unresolved question of his past was deferred until after retirement.

The more of the family tree he discovered, the more living relatives he met, the more old photographs he saw, the more he spoke to me. Here at last was an interest he and I could share: the De Abaituas, our other selves.

In the caravan, he rolls the brandy around his glass then asks me, 'Have you thought about changing your name?'

'Why?'

'Because you've got the wrong name—' he stops to correct himself. 'Not the wrong name, but Humphreys is just the name I chose when I went into the police cadets. It's not your real name.'

Eddie went into the police cadets a gawky, malnourished lad. His grandmother was dead, the house taken over by another relative, and who wants a teenage boy hanging around? The police cadets offered accommodation. His ambitions did not really lie in that direction. He would have liked to draw. But he had no choice. The police or the army. From the cadets, he went to join the police as a constable. Along with the paperwork, he had his birth certificate in a sealed envelope, at this point unaware of its contents. After opening the envelope, the superintendent called him in to explain why he had a birth certificate in another name. He didn't know. His mother had to travel down from Blackpool to explain. Afterwards, he took the name Humphreys by deed poll. A foreign name like De Abaitua would only attract attention in Merseyside Police.

I think of my father as being in possession of the facts and my mother in possession of the fictions. Sylvia was the youngest of five children, the storyteller in the family, and although I have listened to and not forgotten her stories of the past, nor am I convinced that I have got the facts down straight. I am somewhere between fact and fiction.

'Will you change your name?' asks Eddie.

'How do you pronounce it again?'

'Some people say De-a-bay-thua. Some De-a-bite-you-ah.'

And I, who have always been obsessed with alternate selves, am briefly drunkenly fascinated at the prospect of changing my name and becoming somebody else.

Eddie explains that Andrew, my elder brother, cannot change his name because he is already married and has children. And there is no point in my sister changing her name because she will soon be married and take her husband's name. For once, it falls to me, the youngest son, living in this in-between state, neither here nor there, in a remote cottage, to fulfil the family destiny. To fix the broken De Abaitua line and reconnect our lives to the history uncovered by my father's investigations. If I become a De Abaitua then it will be like taking a character from a novel or a figure from a dream and making them real; for Eddie, his son becoming a De Abaitua would be like finally catching a wanted man.

THE DOCK ROAD

Writers are often asked, if you weren't a writer, then who would you be and what would you do for a living?

This question is far trickier than it appears to be.

Frequently, in my adult life, I have not been a writer. I wasn't a writer until I published a novel. Then, not long after its publication, I pretty much stopped being a writer; I worked on a novel one day a week but that was not enough. I continued making notes in journals, plans for potential books that could be written. It became painful after a while, and I wondered if I should let my ambitions dwindle. I had published a novel but failed to commit to the cause of writing, and so it seemed that I would join those ranks of other writers I know who've published this and that and then become food entrepreneurs, teachers, content providers, librarians, or flacks for oligarchs. People for whom writing was a means to an end, or a sacrifice they could not sustain, or an act they simply did not enjoy. People who had everything a writer requires but no luck, or a failure of conviction at the crucial hour. I also know writers who've had enormous success and cannot bear to write again lest they fail to match that success.

There is nothing permanent about being a writer. Because the impulse originates in childhood, it can seem inevitable, but it is also contingent. If I had not gone to work for Will, then I would have been forced to return to Liverpool, and in all likelihood, to my holiday job as a security guard on the Dock Road.

The Dock Road is not marked on maps of Liverpool. But anyone from the city can take you there. The Dock Road encompasses six miles of adjoining streets: if you approach it from the north, from out of the gate of Seaforth Dock, you travel down Shore Road then Waterloo Road, Regent Road, Bath Street and the Strand, taking in the impressive waterfront architecture which includes the Liver Building, and onto Sefton Street in the south. The Dock Road is a state of mind that maps over actual streets. It divides the city from the river, the solidity of the land from the uncertainty of the sea, the boundary between what *is* and what could yet be.

In the summer of 1992, two years before I start work at 1 Hall Cottages, I change trains at Sandhills station, waiting on an exposed platform scoured by the sea wind, overlooking the Dock Road and the turbid Mersey. The river's eel-grey hide turns here and there to show a reptilian white belly. I jog down a steep brick staircase and come into a zone of empty warehouses, bombed-out churches, and desolate, weed-cracked yards; I stride across a box girder bridge, taking in the landmarks: the grey arched bunker of the Tate and Lyle sugar silo, the pumping station of the North Docks, the immense brick tobacco warehouse of Stanley Dock, fourteen storeys high and unthinkably empty.

Overhead, the gulls scorn one another, and then turn on me. I crack them up. I *craaa-kkk, craa-kkk, craaa-kkk* them up. I'm cowled in a black hoodie with a Public Enemy patch on the back, an undergraduate on the look out for authenticity to appropriate, for a desolate, post-industrial wasteland to call my own. I stand outside an empty shop, under a rusting sign showing the sun-bleached Pepsi logo of the previous decade. I walk past a silo and glimpse through the doors men working in the grain dunes and grain valleys, masked and sheathed in chaff, as anonymous and impermanent as snowmen.

I grew up on stories of the Dock Road. Eddie and Sylvia told overlapping tales about it. Liverpool in 1962, the year my father became a policeman, and took up *the job*. Sylvia did not join her sisters screaming at the Beatles at the Cavern, but instead met Eddie for a tentative mope of courtship around the Pier Head. The streets seethed with the human traffic of trade, with all that the ships brought in. Merchant seamen arrive home from Chile or Peru with a gun in one pocket and a tiny monkey in the other, trophies of exotica for the terraced houses of Bootle, Toxteth and Granby. By the 1970s, there were so many parrots going mad in squalid two-up-two-downs that the city could support a parrot psychologist. I remember a particularly foul-mouthed bird self-harming on a perch, pulling out its feathers with the hook of its beak. It had the avian equivalent of male-pattern baldness, if male-pattern baldness was caused by men pulling out tufts of hair because of the interminable suffering of their domestic situation.

I am home for the summer, an undergraduate in need of money. My father pulls a string to get me a job as a security guard. I collect my uniform from Mersey Docks and Harbour Company. He reckons that the experience will be good for me, providing an education in work and other harsh realities.

Eddie started out as a bobby working the Docks. On his very first shift, he was inducted into the dodges of the job by CD, a policeman who had no interest in being a policeman. CD fraternised with the suspects – that is, the dockers and the sailors – and was once found on board a Russian naval submarine playing chess with the crew in defiance of Cold War *froideur* and the armed guard on the gangplank. CD rode around the docks on a bicycle, helmet wobbling because concealed underneath he had hidden a bacon buttie, and eating was forbidden on the job; he was always listening out for the two rings of the night stick that signalled the approach of the inspector. CD went on to become a landlord and millionaire. Eddie, my father, did what he was told. He did *the job*.

Just off the Dock Road, there is a large shop on the second floor of a brick warehouse called 'Just Doors'. It speaks to an urgent obscurity within me, this name, this promise. On the shop floor, dozens of doors stand in a line, so that door opens into door opens into door opens into door. The allure of doorways and river mouths, gateways to new spaces. As if passing through space could be a rite of spiritual passage.

Rites of passage require outlying uninhabited places. Initiates undergoing the rites pass through the status of outcast. Mary Douglas, the great anthropologist, observed that rites of passage are often made to sound more dangerous than they actually are. Danger, she noted, lies in transitional states, being neither one thing nor another, that condition of in-betweenness and unbelonging. In *Purity and Danger*, she writes, 'To say the boys risk their lives says precisely that to go out of the formal structure and to enter the margins is to be exposed to power that is enough to kill them or to make their manhood.'

As an interzone between the land and the sea, between form

and formlessness, the docks are perfect for an initiation rite.

For my first shift as a security guard, my mother drives me north up the Dock Road to Seaforth container dock. My uniform is a peaked cap, a clip-on tie, black polyester trousers and a blue shirt with epaulettes on it. At school, I often wore surplus police shirts from which my mother had clipped the epaulettes, leaving tell-tale holes at the collarbone which marked me out to teachers and my fellow pupils as the copper's son. Normally, Neptune Security did not accept someone as young as myself as a security guard. However, as the son of a high-ranking police officer, they know that I can be trusted.

At the dock gate, I wave goodbye to my mother, and am issued with a yellow hard hat and directed to a Portakabin. There, the senior guard, in beard and glasses and high-visibility jacket, allocates me the gangplank of a container ship for my first shift. The ship's insurance demands the presence of a guard. The first Gulf war is over but the possibility of terrorism remains. He hitches up his trousers, which are caught in the fat man's paradox, the waist too narrow to encompass the gut but too wide to hang on the hips, then gives me a clipboard to note down the names of the sailors who come and go.

The shift is twelve hours long. I must stand on the gangplank of a giant container freighter from seven at night until seven in the morning. No sitting down, no reading. After about half-an-hour, a young seaman in a boiler suit saunters by; he's a lad about my age, and I see – in his grimy, tanned expression, in the raising of his oil-flecked blonde eyebrows – that he's wondering where I went wrong in life to merit such a lowly and punishing position.

The sun sets over container stacks. A distant klaxon wails and here come the straddle carriers. I've been warned about this. How dangerous it is to be out when the straddle carriers are working. They are forty-foot-tall cranes that race around on their wheeled stilts, fetching containers from the bays and depositing them on the quay for a large stately crane to load onto the freighter.

The scale of the docks is exhilarating. Deep oily waters lap against immense cold iron hulls. But the boredom of standing on the gangplank, overlooking the quiet floodlit quay, is quite painful. Hour after hour is extracted from me without sedation.

The gangplank is a riveted iron ramp. I try to take the names of the sailors but they wave me away. I'm denied even that tiny task. My undergraduate egotism squirms under this uniformed anonymity. I am a piece of human signage, I am small print. It is clearly the most-hated shift, and as the new boy it is my induction into the profession. Induction or warning. I want to thrive in the docks as my father had before me. To make my manhood in this place. More than that, I want to belong to Liverpool, for I was raised at the periphery of the city and know nothing of the life at its heart.

But the Dock Road is a dead heart. It is mile after mile of rain-soaked cobbles, potholes and empty warehouses. Gone are the throng of flat-capped dockers and their dock hooks, gone are the sailors of every stripe on shore leave, gone are the barrow women selling fruit and veg, gone are the dray horses pulling their burdens. Ghosts, with their heads down and hands shoved deep in coat pockets, trudge from gate to gate in search of work. The pubs are mostly empty. Gone are the landladies in fox furs with lipstick-tipped ciggies, gone are the whalers' brawls that spill from bar to lounge. No more seaman's business done upstairs at the Pig and Whistle over a pie and a pint. No more rites of passage. How can I make my manhood in a place that has been so systematically unmanned?

On his first shift at the docks, Eddie worked the gate,

searching the taxis bringing the sailors back after shore leave. Prostitutes would stow themselves in the boot of the cab with the intention of working a long shift with the men confined to quarters. Like my father, I also had my orders to prevent any prostitutes from entering the ship. These orders are quickly modified in an aside from another guard: they all have a thing going with the girls so I'm either to accept a sexual favour from the women or four cans of beer in return for letting them through. He infers that participating in this corruption will make me a man; that is, induct me in the *real* job. My education in the Dock Road entails fieldwork in *the real world*, that euphemism for the trade of minds and bodies for money, the selling of time and labour in return for capital's meagre offering. I stand on the gangplank of the ship and wonder, where would this whore's blow job take place? Around the back of the Portakabin perhaps, for the stimulation and amusement of the other guards, or just beyond the amber floodlights of the quay, reclining awkwardly in the coil of an iron chain as she performs the act that finally inducts me into the corruption of adulthood. No, this is not the rite I seek. Anyway, it's moot. No prostitutes come clacking up the gangplank. I loiter in the entrance of the ship, a writer without a pen, devising scenarios, plotting them out, forgetting them.

At midnight, the floodlights are turned up. The dockers begin to load luxury sports cars onto the freighter. They can't resist a quick spin around the quay in the cars, giving it full throttle, windows down, whooping and yowling, and we all cheer as they rattle the Ferraris and Porsches at a fair old clip up the gang plank. Daredevil driving is a perk of the job. The cars are all loaded, the floodlights dim, the night returns heavier than before.

The last three hours are the heaviest. Four o'clock in the

morning goes on forever. Part of me will always be standing on that gangplank, unable to move onward through time. Head nodding, foot-sore and mentally burnt-out. At dawn, the return of the almost-forgotten sun. I hold my palms out to the first blush of heat. Far out in the widening river and beneath gilded clouds, gulls form an arch as they fly from one sandbank to another. I feel their flight intensely, and I'm choked with envy. Now I know why they refer to the changing of shifts as 'the relief'. I experience a relief so intense it is a kind of ecstasy.

When the shift is over, I return to Sandhills station, walking in my stinking uniform against rush hour, cap concealed in a plastic bag. On the train, it's an effort to stay awake for the commute back home, head lolling in time to the rolling stock.

Then, after a morning's kip, curtains drawn against a hot sun, no sooner have I rubbed the stiffness out of my calves then I am driven back to the docks by my mother for another shift, another course of correction. I pick up my hardhat at the gate, and arrive at the Portakabin for my assignment. Another gangplank. A small ship this time. No chair, no book. A different senior guard, a lean older man, a father or grandfather, who takes pity on me and collects me every hour for a cup of tea and ten minutes in the Portakabin. The previous shift was crammed with novelty and distraction compared to this one. I scratch around the same four yards of rickety gangplank, and try to think myself out of existence.

A uniform erases the self; that is its purpose. To replace individual judgment with the consensus of the profession. This is how Eddie explains the law to me, when I ask whether he feels guilty about arresting people whose crimes are really a function of their economic status.

'Democratically-elected politicians decide the law. I enforce the law. If I question the law, then I am going against democracy.'

Eddie was proud to wear the uniform of a copper, with his heavy truncheon and night stick, hard tall helmet and bovver boots. He stood for the law. You can disappear behind the law. You can become the uniform. But you don't want to become the uniform of a security guard. A security guard is just furniture, his uniform is upholstery.

Let's do the maths. Twelve hour shifts at three pounds an hour. Four shifts a week, sometimes less, sometimes more. The family men get first choice. The men supporting wives and children on six twelve-hour shifts a week at three pounds an hour. Men like Terry, with whom I share a night lunch in the Portakabin. Always the filthy seat covers, creaking busted sofas and chairs, stale fag smoke and softcore pornography: in my experience, Portakabins lack a woman's touch. We delicately unwrap our homemade sandwiches. Terry has corned beef and ketchup, a packet of salt 'n' vinegar crisps and a can of Coke, his one luxury.

'Your one luxury?' I ask.

He does the maths.

'Three pounds an hour. Twelve hours a shift. Six shifts a week. Taxman takes his lump. National Insurance. Then the missus and her kid take their lump. End of that, I only have enough money left to buy me packed lunch. I don't need the can of Coke. I could do without the Coke.'

'It's not essential.'

'Right. But it keeps me awake on the night shifts. And I like it.'

At his right hand, he keeps a packet of twenty Embassy filters, short strong cigarettes designed for a working man to suck down between tasks, as opposed to the extra-long Superkings that are fit only for idlers, a baton of a fag to savour while watching telly.

Two peaked caps set aside on a melamine table. It is long after midnight and long before dawn: Terry and I assume the role of bad mentor and unwilling pupil. Either Terry is unconvinced that I fully appreciate the tragic mathematics of his situation, or we have plenty of time for him to go over it again.

'Her kid needs stuff. There are bills to pay. All that is left over for me is *this*.'

The can of Coke, which I watch him drain sip-by-sip. The cigarettes, which he does not share. He asks me about university. I explain that I am a student in English Literature. That I read books. Novels, poetry, criticism, history, psychology, philosophy.

'What's the point of that?'

'I want to be a writer.'

Terry is angry with students, believing they should know something of the real world (a domain which excludes novels, poetry, criticism, history, psychology, philosophy, but includes economics). He forgives me my various indiscretions with books because at least I've got off my arse to do a proper job.

When summer is over, I will return to my studies. He will remain on the docks. That is *that*. Terry serves up the story of his life as a cautionary tale, and I am a nodding witness to his heroic struggle just to keep going.

Another shift, a change of duties. I am sent out to the bays to check the seals on the containers. The seals are individually numbered and I yank at them to ensure they are intact and that the numbers imprinted on them match the ones on my clipboard. The supervisor insists I wear my high-visibility jacket.

'You have to be careful,' he says.

'Why?'

'The bays are where the straddle carriers work. When the ship is in, they are under pressure to move the containers as quickly as they can. The cranes go forty miles an hour. The drivers of the straddle carriers are forty feet up, and they can't see you.'

'How will I know when they are coming?'

'As soon as you hear a klaxon, abandon your post, and make for the safety of the Portakabin.'

The docks smell of grain and malt and diesel, not an unpleasant smell, but one I will always associate with them; that, and the noxious interaction between polyester and the human body. Out on the bays, tugging at the seals, noting down their numbers, I'm happy to have something to do in the general rounds of dock life.

It was the move to container freight that killed the docks. Once the freight could be stacked in sealed boxes, loaded and unloaded by straddle carrier and crane, there was no need for a mass unionised workforce. Especially one as troublesome as the dockers. In '92, the remaining dockers had not entirely knuckled down; their last strike – a gesture that marked, for the world at large, the absolute victory of capital – lay a couple of years in the future.

The containers also made it more difficult for the casual pilfering of the old days; Eddie tells me stories of dockers coming to work with fake paunches made from newspaper, so that when they left at the end of the shift, they could wrap their lean bellies in bolts of stolen cotton and nothing would seem amiss to the bobbies. Now and again, customs officers crack a container, and I stand guard as the possessions of some family are stacked up on a warehouse while the sniffer dogs make their way up and over the goods. Liverpool's reputation for stealing starts at the docks. The cross-country network for fencing stolen goods, established by Liverpool criminals after the war, became the drug distribution network in the Eighties and Nineties. Liverpool criminals always travelled. Not for them the turf wars of the London gangsters. Eddie will collar Scousers in Amsterdam and Africa, USA, Germany and Spain. Assassins from the South American drug cartels will kill on the streets of Toxteth.

The containers are stacked three high. Of course, I can only check the ones on the ground. What if the thief has a ladder? That's not unheard of, is it?

I am recording the number of a seal when the klaxon goes, echoing across the quay, and the straddle carriers speed toward the bay in formation. I run along the tight corrugated slivers between the containers, a gap just wide enough for a man or for the leg of a straddle carrier, but not for both at the same time. It's my first taste of danger on the docks. It will not be my last.

A few days later, I arrive for my next shift, but all is quiet. Work has stopped. A straddle carrier has overturned, killing the docker driving it. The men have time off to attend his funeral. First, it's breakfast. The dockers take me in, and for a couple of quid, one of them makes me a fine and full English breakfast. (Later that evening, when I am praising the generosity of the dockers to Eddie, he mimes a thief quietly pilfering a container while I fill my guileless belly). A grey-whiskered docker takes an interest in my copy of AS Byatt's *Possession*.

'What's it about?' he asks.

'Romance. Poetry. Victorian literature.'

'Are you political?' he asks.

'Yes,' I reply.

'Which newspaper do you read?'

'The *Daily Mirror* of a weekend, the *Guardian* in the week. Left-wing papers.'

'They're not left-wing papers,' he says. He hands me a copy of the *Morning Star*.

'*That's* a left-wing paper.'

He wants to know what they teach me at university. What do I learn about the real world, which for him encompasses the workers' struggle, Karl Marx and socialism? What do they teach me about the exploitation of labour by the forces of capital?

It turns out that I know far less about politics than I thought. 'You need a real education, mate,' he says, laughing.

When I come out of the Portakabin with the dockers, and see the other security guards loitering and smoking over by their hut, I realised I've crossed a line between opposing camps, between the way things were and the way things will be: with their temporary contracts and irregular and long shifts, the security guards are hapless prophecies of the future. Whereas the dockers, with their insistence on worker's rights, reasonable remuneration and pride in the job, are *fucking dinosaurs*.

Hourly night patrol through the timber yards of Huskisson Dock, one of the North docks on the eastern side of the River Mersey. A lonely shift in a two-storey Portakabin but it comes with perks. I am permitted a radio and I am allowed to write. I set out my desk as if I am working at the university library, with pen, and foolscap pad and my copy of *Possession*. In the filing cabinet, I discover a pile of communal softcore pornography for the other security guards who work this shift. Piles of porn crop up at various Portakabins, and after the other guards snipe about my choice of reading matter, I take to sheathing my copy of *Possession* in a careworn edition of *Knave*.

The other guards confide their peeping tom stories to me, the frozen acts of intercourse caught in the beam of their Maglite, a white arse between splayed thighs. If one believes the letters page of *Knave*, security guards get a lot of casual sex. In reality, it's a long, solitary job, and being able to masturbate during a shift is described by one colleague as 'a perk'. (Later, the same guard confides in me the erotic frisson he gets from using security cameras to zoom in and follow women walking across a car park – perfect, if grainy black-and-white images of women searching their handbags for car keys are your thing.)

On Huskisson Dock, there's no supervisor but still I undertake and log my night patrols. A cold fog drifts over the Mersey, the secrets of the sea which cannot be wholly contained within the steep-sided berths of the dock. The dock edge is not fenced off. In the past, when the city suffered from smogs, the dockers and seamen crawled around on their hands and knees lest they take a lethal step over the edge. I flash the torch around, discovering where the cobbled yard ends and the cold black absence of the water begins. In the timber warehouse, footsteps echo high up in the rafters like the rolling of giant bone dice. The beam from the long-handled Maglite flashes here and there, down and up, revealing stacks and timber and empty pallets, the silvery glimmer of cobwebs and the blank spots in the eyes of roosting pigeons. Some night patrols take me to the river's edge where large hewn boulders form a defence against a rising tide. Rats move in the angular shadows between the rocks then plop back into the water. Under the dark toil of its contrary current, the Mersey is a black twisting void. Formlessness. Death. Fear sharpens the moment. I walk back along the cobbles to the Portakabin. Check that it is empty, that I am still alone. The radio breaks the threat of silence.

I set to work. In my notepad, I write of bombed-out churches and abandoned pubs and the collapsed warehouses of the Dock Road, populated by birdmen in diesel-smeared dungarees. Because I know nothing of the real world, I write hallucinations: the brooding brick war mask of the Anglican cathedral, a dead pale heart lifted by crane from the crypt, the organist welding chords as the priest cranks up the engines of faith to calculate the number of the beast…hallucinations of the industrial gothic, the horrors that lurk in rotten machines. From the Dock Road to the twin cathedrals of Hope Street, a zone where religion and organised labour rust into one amorphous mound of spoil. I don't write about people. I can't write about things as they are.

My shifts take me all over the city. The senior guards drive me around in a little van to two or three postings a night. In Fazakerley, an all-night garage is plagued by an armed robber. He's been sticking the barrel of his gun through the rectangular gap used for transactions. If anyone sticks a gun barrel through the porthole, I am to grab it.

The garage is secured within a cage of chicken wire. The attendant is a lad about my age called Spider. He prefers the name Tom but the wastrels who drift in on the night currents know him as Spider, the younger brother of someone notorious. The punters are taxi drivers, clubbers and junkies. The junkies buy KitKats for the silver foil and abandon the chocolate wafers by the petrol pump. Spider brings his stereo into work. He introduces me to John Lee Hooker, and electrified blues will never sound as good as they did booming across the forecourt in another endless four in the morning.

A briny, oily wind blows in through the porthole. As long as we do not leave the cage, and take a dip in the treachery outside, we should be fine. I have a stick that is a yard long, cored-out, and filled with lead ball bearings. Spider has stencilled Knucklebreaker down the side of it. I thrum with anticipation that one of the junkies will make a grab for him, a grab for the till, and then I will take up Knucklebreaker and strike the errant hands again and again so that the blood licks up against the Perspex partition, and I will at last commit the required corruption of manhood.

The van comes to take me away. We drive to the club house in Formby where the alarm is ringing, and the burglars may still be on the job. I am young and strong and green and sent in first. The handle of the Maglite is long so that I can use it to open a closed door at a marginally safe distance. In the ballroom of the club house, anticipating burglars unscrewing the chandelier, I barge through the door and come suddenly face-to-face with a terrifying full-length reflection of myself. The lot of the free-range security guard is boredom enlivened by brief outbreaks of terror, like one of Stalin's dinner parties.

Nights on the Dock Road, life worn so thin that phantoms and memories can be discerned through the stretched weave.

The real horrors come in the day shifts. The slums in the Dingle. The watchful silent faces of children at the windows of a tower block who torch cars and, when the fire engines arrive, throw stones at the firemen. Dropped off at B&Q, I apprehend children stealing duvet covers; in the garden section, the kids have constructed a see-saw which they use to catapult the duvet covers over the twelve-foot fence and into the hands of older brothers on the other side, to be hawked on the market or down the pub. Three men run through the queues at the till carrying a set of patio doors, and the staff and security spill after them. A brawl in the car park ensues, one of the thieves is a wanted man and he's full of Scotch. But I miss this fight, as it happened the week before, so I only get to hear stories about it.

My final shift is at a nightclub after closing time. The management have suffered a few thefts and suspect punters are going into the club then hiding on the premises to rob the place once the staff have gone home. The supervisor drops me at the door. It's the kind of club I went to before I was a student, a modest pick-up joint, double Southern Comfort for the price of a single, your best pulling shirt and a bouncer who specialises in the inspection of smart shoes. Maglite out, I check the toilets, first the men's, cubicle by cubicle, and then the ladies, with its distinctive brew of perfume, bare feet in high heels, fag smoke and the bilious whiff of regurgitated Bacardi. Laddered stockings half-in, half-out of a swing-top bin. The tiles are damp from the dry ice and the dancing. The party is over, and that is my cue.

I find a clean table, and resume writing. But I am nineteen years old and once I've exhausted the adrenalised vibe of the early hours, there is not much else I have to say. I finish reading *Possession* instead, and then, for the first time, I fall asleep on the job. If I was smart I would have crawled under the table or slept behind the bar. No, I slump head first right in the window of the bar. My supervisor wakes me in the grey dawn with a sharp rap against the glass. My time is up.

The Dock Road promised me a rite of passage. The making of my manhood. I'm not talking about sex, I lost my virginity long ago. Is it violence I want? One time, I was guarding the gangplank of a naval supply ship and a couple of dockers wanted to come on board. The naval ships are known for their decent canteen, and the dockers were on the blag, pretending to be ex-naval so that they could talk their way into a roast dinner or two. An officer asked me to eject a pair of them, but they went amenably enough. This was the closest I came to proving my manhood. It was exactly as Mary Douglas predicted: the docks provided rites that were surrounded with the aura of danger but were, in themselves, quite harmless.

In August, I move back to York University in anticipation of a second year of studies. In the week before term, my friends and I are walking across the sports fields. Late summer afternoon, the prospect of lazy drinks in the college bar. The six of us – four men, two women – walk along the markings of the cricket pitch when my hackles rise. Up by the cricket hut, there are twenty or thirty local lads. We feel their presence at our backs. They say a few things, we keep walking. And then one of them throws a battery, and it lands at El's feet and I make the mistake of turning around. Because how can you not turn around when a man throws a battery at you? My friends are outraged at my mistake, my turning around to face trouble.

One of the lads runs full pelt down the hill and in one smooth movement punches me hard in the face. My lip is split. I am shocked but I am not hurt. My friends don't fare so well, and go down under kicks and punches. I pull a few lads off them, and then I have to make the decision to punch a lad in the face. I punch him just hard enough to shock him but not so hard as to incite reprisals.

'Stop this!' I shout. 'It's pointless!'

My mouth is full of blood but I'm not even angry. This is my true rite of passage: punched in the face I remain eminently reasonable. That is what marks me out as ready for the middle class: that I can defer gratification, stifle fury, for some putative future gain. I may be six foot two, fourteen stone of muscle and one stone of fat, but I will never be good at fighting because I will always have to calculate whether to hit back or not. Because there is no aspect of my life that a brawl improves, no problem that can be solved with violence. And yet, as a young man, you give up that aspect of your persona reluctantly, want to hint that you can put yourself about. Eddie could dish it out. In the riot at Cantril Farm, he fought hand-to-hand against the rioters for hours.

After the brawl, my friend's tooth is chipped. My face looks far worse than it is. No lasting harm done. We will endure.

That's what I learned on the gangplank of the ship. Endurance. Life in the real world. I can't dish it out but I can take it.

THE SIZEWELL CURE

The day after my father asked me to change my name, I have a punishing beer-and-brandy hangover, and scuttle around 1 Hall Cottages readying the place for Will's return. He is due back from Brazil and I want everything to be ready for him. All transcriptions printed out, messages carefully noted on the pad, laundry done, and car repaired. A single item remains on the to-do list: the gas line on the front of the house. The gasman is booked but will not arrive for a couple of days.

I disposed of the ducks without decoding their meaning. Col insisted that he had nothing to do with them. But he might have been having fun at my expense, trying to spook me. During the preparations for Will's arrival, Col appears at the front gate. Finally, he has decided to own up about the ducks.

I walk down the garden path.

'What can I help you with, Col?' I ask.

He doesn't face me. He looks out over the field – the landscape is as worthy of his attention as our conversation.

'I thought I should tell you something,' he says. Here we go. Ducks.

'Have you seen anyone lurking around here?' he asks.

'I haven't seen anyone.'

'Nothing suspicious?'

'Like two dead ducks appearing on a keyboard?'

'Because somebody has been at the pheasants.' Now he looks at me. His remark catches me by surprise. I had thought that what went on with the pheasants was strictly between me and the animal kingdom. I try to master my expression but it's too late. My face has already expressed.

'Maybe it was a fox,' I suggest.

Col shakes his head, uses his tongue to work the unlit dog-end from one corner of his mouth to the other so that he can light it.

'It was a clean cut,' he demonstrates with a cutting motion of his hand.

I'm briefly lost in thought concerning Col's aptitude in the gathering of forensic evidence. The axe is still in the shed, propped up beside my bike.

'Why would someone kill a pheasant?' I ask.

'Psychopaths start on animals, that's what they say. You might want to lock your door at night.'

How would he know that we keep our door unlocked unless it was him who sneaked in and dropped the ducks on the keyboard?

I ask Col, 'Have you spoken to the man next door about the pheasant?'

We both regard 2 Hall Cottages. The inhabitant keeps himself to himself. Will has been inside. He told me the man who lives there has stacked the furniture up in a disturbing way. He only lives on one floor of the cottage. I have seen the man's car now and again and grunted acknowledgment when our paths crossed at the front of the cottages.

'He's been here longer than you two. We've never had any trouble from him.'

Deadlocked in mutual suspicion, me thinking about the ducks, him thinking about the pheasant, I back away and return to the cottage.

Will doesn't call to tell me when to expect him, but I expect him nonetheless. I light the garden flares, lay in some Scotch and stock up the fridge. I sit on the sofa listening to the radio. I am the dog that longs for its master, nervously haunting the hallway and wandering the front lawn at night, looking out across the field for approaching headlights suffusing the distant hedgerows.

He does not come.

I repeat the ritual the next day. The garden flares are landing lights for the lost traveller. As much as I want him to return, I am also nervous of him; we had a couple of weeks together and that was it, I don't really know him at all. And he is my employer. What if he fires me? What if he lets me go? I have no plan B.

The flares to welcome him home burn out. Past midnight, but I'm still awake with anxiety. And then a cab pulls up outside the cottage. He arrives into darkness. He mumbles a question: *why are you up?* I have so much to say to him, stories and messages and minor achievements in his cause that I have secured, but he has been in London and *on it*. He is not interested and this lack of interest extends even to his own coherence. His eyes turn independently of one another, reluctant to focus on the place he has returned to, the place of no fun and no interest.

'Don't wake me in the morning,' he growls.

Instructions are good. Even ones as mean-tempered as this. Instructions mean I still have a role to play and have not yet been cast back into my fate as an entirely unnecessary young man.

Unfortunately, the next morning, the gas man arrives at nine sharp to move the gas line from the front of the house. The gas man is an Australian with a blonde ponytail.

'Please could you work quietly,' I say to him. 'The boss is in bed. He's a bit the worse for wear. I'd really appreciate it if you didn't wake him.'

The gas man looks sceptical. My warning gives him pause. He didn't expect that. And the cottage is quite remote.

'I will have to use the drill,' he says.

'Could you drill quietly? I'd just really appreciate it if the boss could sleep in.'

The gas man nods, but not in agreement, merely in acknowledgment that he has heard me but is not prepared to do anything about it. The waking of the boss is not his problem.

Drilling, hammering, clanging ensue. Nervously, I pace around the living room listening for signs of life from upstairs. I make three cups of tea to interrupt the work but the whirring, the banging, the blasting continue. I take a cup upstairs. Smoke from the special cigarette seeps from under the bedroom door. I leave the tea outside.

'You woke him,' I say to the gas man. His ponytail flicks indifferently as he continues with the work then, finally, he gives in to my offer of tea. We retire to the living room. The gas man talks about surfing while I listen anxiously to the creaking of the bed upstairs and the sound of large footsteps padding across the bedroom floor. A door bangs open. The gas man flinches slightly. But from his expression I can see that he finds the situation ridiculous. To be afraid of waking up some man!

And then Will appears at the top of the stairs, naked, apart from a towel, which is draped over his head. The gas man squeaks, a quite unexpected sound to come from a grown man, that palpable squeak. Will's tattoos on his arms are blocky abstract shapes because they have been overwritten. But the eye is quickly drawn away from his body to apprehend the awful spectacle of his face. What has happened to his face? The gas man sets his tea down on a table. He is about to make a run for it. But first, one last look at Will's face. It is disturbingly swollen into a terrible topography of distorted features each topped with welts and scratches.

Will treads deliberately, nakedly, down the stairs.

'I've been scratching at my face all night,' he says. 'Opiates give me image horror. Now my face is infected.'

This explanation does not reassure the gas man. He moves briskly at a crouch into the garden.

Will turns his swollen eye to me. He has become the man lost *In the Land of Retinal Delights*, one great staring eye distorting the side of his face.

Will says, 'I have a plan to deal with my face. I am going to take the Sizewell cure. Get your trunks.' With that he hands me an empty mug, retrieves clothing from his suitcase, and goes back upstairs.

Four and a half miles from the cottage, the twin nuclear power stations of Sizewell dominate the Suffolk coastline. Sizewell A is a functional concrete box next to the dome of tessellated white tiles that is Sizewell B.

The waters around Sizewell are tropically warm, as seawater is pumped in to cool the reactor and then vented back into the North Sea. The visitors' centre offers the reassurance that the radioactive waste produced by the reactor is very small in weight and height compared to the waste produced by coal, which is very large.

While Will dresses, I mollify the gas man with sugary tea and a honk on the special cigarette. Will joins us for banter, and then he and I undertake the walk to Sizewell. As instructed I have trunks and towels, but I am also bringing along the frying pan, some potatoes and sausages to cook dinner. Will walks quickly. I stalk after him across the flatlands, trying to keep pace. We don't talk much until we reach a house within sight and sound of the reactors. The house is empty and up for rent. In the back garden, the thrumming from deep inside the nuclear reactors is not merely audible – it is loud. A pylon stands astride the house. Its thick wire sizzles in the damp air. The dusk is heavy with static and mad electrified thought.

'We should live here,' says Will.

Mapless, we press on. The beach is on the other side of the reactor complex. We try to find a shortcut, then Will suggests bunking over the fence into the nuclear reactor.

My job as Will Self's amanuensis requires a relentless willingness to participate in the unusual. The only way I can survive as a passenger on this brief journey we are on together, not merely as a metaphorical passenger but also as an actual passenger during his deranged bouts of driving, the only way I can get through all this without losing my nerve and crying and demanding to be let out, is to have the courage of his convictions. But just because I am a grunt, enlisted in a very small and embattled infantry division, in which Will Self is the sergeant major, does not mean that I will break into a nuclear power reactor with a pair of trunks and some sausages, and a man with a mutated face, just so he can take a short cut to the beach.

No way.

Not unless he insists upon it.

Reason prevails. We walk around the perimeter.

On the beach, the waves obsessive-compulsively arrange and rearrange the pebbles. There is a point equidistant between Sizewell and the sea where the sound of the churning reactor and the noisy sorting of the beach overlap, and there I stand and sway.

The sea merges into a mackerel sky, fillets of cloud laid side by side with clear blue pools between, like the meres of the bird reserve with their bulrushes and whicker-whisper in the sea breeze. Will points to the pumping station out in the water, a derelict-looking rig and a hang-out for gulls. He walks into the sea, and I follow him: we swim out to the rig until the water becomes as warm as a stream of irradiated piss. This is how we take the Sizewell cure. It works. The swelling on his face comes down, revealing an expression I cannot hope to decipher. Regret? Guilt? Craving?

We gather driftwood for a campfire. Driftwood burns ferociously and Will does not stop loading it onto the fire. As mere infantry, I have no authority to ask him to stop. Our campfire becomes a blazing beacon and then I am instructed to cook upon it. The frying pan catches fire as soon as I place it on the conflagration; the oil burns, the sausages burn, the silver foil fuses with the potatoes to form a sort of vegetable cyborg: there will be no food tonight.

The fire is so hot that the pebbles underneath pop and crack. Will is silent. The fire in the night expresses his fury in a way I am too young to understand. I am very much on the outside of his story whereas he is at the centre of mine.

When the fire subsides, I talk about the visit of Eddie and Sylvia, and then I remember that Eddie had asked me to change my name.

'What to?' asks Will. He has a professional interest in names. A few people still believe Will Self to be a pseudonym.

'De Abaitua,' I say and I spell it out. 'It's Basque. I come from a short line of Liverpool Basques. It should have been my name, but it wasn't because my Dad changed it when he was young. Now he wants me to change it back.'

'What does De Abaitua mean?'

'It means "from the land of plenty". My ancestors must have appeared well-fed.'

'Names are very important,' says Will. 'Vital, even. Crucial. And it's a much better name than Humphreys isn't it?'

I nod. I have always hated the name Humphreys.

'It's decided,' says Will, deciding. 'From now on, I will introduce you as Matthew De Abaitua to everyone you meet.'

The breaking surf is luminescent under the moon. The wood in the campfire seethes and our shadows slide over the pebbles. The shadow: the ancient metaphor for the other self, the person you might have been, the dark you, the doppelgänger with the same face but a different name. I say yes, that's who I will be. I don't have to think twice.

* * *

Normal life in the cottage resumes. I give my report of goings on in Will's absence, reading through each phone message and reporting on progress made. He interrupts me: 'Did you get any ducks?' he asks.

'You know about them?'

'Yes. There was a broken-down van. I gave them a hand. The men had been out shooting and said they'd drop us a pair of birds by way of thanks.'

'I got the ducks, yes.'

Back in the office, I pick up an old copy of the *Idler* with Homer Simpson on the cover. The magazine contains an interview with Will Self conducted by the editor Tom Hodgkinson. Puffing away on the special cigarette, Will Self riffs on boredom, motorways and the Citroën DSA. The *Idler* generation itself he dismisses as being demographically insignificant compared to the baby boomers.

I look up. 'But don't you think that the rave movement is meaningful?' I say to him.

He tuts.

'It's simple numbers. Your generation are few and therefore economically insignificant compared to my generation. You are redundant. Your interests and art will never attract a significant audience.'

He takes the copy of the *Idler* from me, and points emphatically at the pages.

'*These* are precisely the type of people you should be associating with, if you want to get on. Oxbridge. Bright young literary types. You must have a plan if you want to write.'

'Did you have a plan?'

'I was not ignorant of certain realities.' He takes out a copy of Granta's *Best Young British Novelists*, a list he appeared on prior to the publication of his first novel *My Idea of Fun*. In the group photograph of the writers, Will's brooding countenance stands out: he is posed off to the right puffing on a cigar, part of the gang but still apart from the gang.

'The *Idler* is where you start. Write something on spec and I will fax it to them.'

I write about my summer job as a security guard on Liverpool docks and how, at sunrise, I had watched the gulls fly in a silhouetted arc from one sandbank to another and vowed never to work a proper job again.

My article for the *Idler* is titled 'Time is all we own'. In a job, I argue, we exchange the commodity we have in abundance – time – for one that is scarce – money. But when we are old and time is scarce we will not be able to pay to get those hours back. The time-money exchange goes strictly one-way. This observation – so commonplace it barely merits mentioning – is tricked out with anecdotes from the docks and languorous scenes from the pylon-stalked plains of Suffolk. At the bottom of the article I type out my new name: Matthew De Abaitua.

Will signs my *Idler* article with his Mont Blanc fountain pen – 'Tom, this is the piece I told you about', W and then in brackets (Self) – and files it by fax. I fiddle with my puzzle ring and wait. How long will the *Idler* take to respond to an unsolicited contribution?

Because it's signed by Will Self, they get to it double-quick. About two weeks later, the editor Tom Hodgkinson calls and asks to speak to me. He likes the piece and will pay me fifty pounds for it. Zed the photographer and his assistant will drive down to Suffolk and photograph my silhouette against the sea mist on the pebbled beach at Sizewell. It is the beginning of a career, albeit career in the sense of a swift, uncontrolled rush.

* * *

Will spends his birthday in the cottage. I give him a VHS of Tarkovsky's *Solaris* to watch when he is next in London. Victoria has bought him a pullover, a knitted patterned thing, and he strides around the cottage wearing it, while I mash some opium heads for Horlicks Plus. Bugs leap for freedom out of the boiling water. It's a good-natured evening and I suspect Will has treated himself to a cheeky half. He keeps disappearing into his study then emerging with a different Italian typewriter in its smooth dust cover. He adores the tactility of the typewriters, showing them off to me and lauding their virtues, their lovable vices, as if they were cats. Then the tactile allure of the pullover becomes quite distracting. Will abrades its wool between his fingers.

'Pullover,' he says. 'Pully. Lovely pully. Love your pully.'

The next morning, Will wakes refreshed. He takes down the last of the flypaper and prepares for another long trip, this time to Australia.

NELSON & EL

In the cottage, the brass pipes lament the filling of the bath. The mould on the window frame advances another spotted inch. How long have I been on my own this time? Days? Weeks.

I slide into the bath and feel its grit. There is no shower curtain so I don't use the rubber shower attachment, and fling its bloodless, tangled guts into the corner of the bathroom. My personal hygiene is not what it could be. I seem to have reverted to the one-bath-a-week routine of my childhood. However, as I am expecting guests, I must make some effort to clean up my act.

Guests. The thought of guests is arousing. The head of my penis slowly breaks the surface of the bath water; it is an opium poppy reared in Martian soil, heavy with narcotic sensation. My blood flows thick and fast with desire, and I want to keep it that way. I like the urgency of wanting. It makes things happen.

Over the next three days, I expect two guests. El and Nelson.

Nelson will arrive first, travelling down from Oldham, where he works in a pub. Nelson and I grew up together in Maghull. He has been recording conversations at the bar on his Dictaphone and posting the cassettes to me. I have been transcribing them for my own purposes. Nelson is not going to be a writer himself. At university, he dallied with the works of Kerouac and Jim Morrison, and would play and rewind, play and rewind the first few bars of 'When The Music's Over' on the stereo of his white Fiesta as we roared around the edgelands of Lancashire. But Nelson went to the University of Madchester and education-wise that was that.

In his first year, dancing at the Haçienda in the hot zone of the Madchester outbreak, Nelson and eleven other lads formed a cohort of excess. Only two of them made it through to the second year. Drink and drugs propagate themselves in their hosts, becoming an irresistible contagion of bad ideas. Amphetamine psychosis – it's catching. I slept in a room abandoned by one housemate, a kickboxing skinhead, and the walls had been scored by his fingernails. The skinhead was last seen ripping the heads off pigeons outside the Arndale Centre. He is still out there and could return at any moment, bald head sticky with bloody feathers, to reclaim his room. Nelson had to take a year off to pull himself together, and now he works in a pub. That was that.

The postman pooters down Church Road. The gate rattles. Padded envelopes containing proof copies of other people's novels thump onto the mat. Among these and many stiff card invitations to openings and launches, there is a postcard from Will in Australia. On one side there is a photograph of a koala with a few facts about the bear: it seldom drinks, for example, and Will has highlighted this section to draw attention to my dissimilarity to it in this regard. I turn the card over. 'Dear Matt, This beast resembles you physically but not in terms of its habits. Keep your pecker up. Will.'

My pecker is up. Like Chekhov's gun: if you introduce a pecker in the first act then the pecker must go off in the third.

Will is deep in the Outback. His exploration of Aboriginal politics and magic has him spooked. He leans on his contact out in Australia to tell him more about the Aboriginal use of sympathetic magic, and he replies that he is absolutely and totally terrified about the whole business.

Will says, 'They told him that they would take him to the place where the trees bleed.' The phone line crackles and it's hard for me to understand what Will is talking about.

I ask, 'Metaphorical trees, you mean.'

'No. Real trees. Real blood. I shouldn't be talking about it,' he says, and he ends the call.

Sympathetic magic is the belief that the manipulation of symbols can influence the event or person that symbol represents. Will wonders if the Aboriginal witch doctors are using sympathetic magic for political ends, putting stardust in the eyes of the politicians they wish to manipulate, gaining back a significant portion of the lost land. In the cottage, Will keeps his distance from the occult experimentation of Bryon Gysin and William Burroughs, filing it under madness, symptoms thereof. I thought I was more susceptible than Will to this kind of talk, with the cut-ups and my experiments in hypnagogic sleep. But it seems we are both inclined to mysticism. Isn't there something magical in our fascination with names, and the sense that the name can influence the thing that it represents? Haven't I just changed my name?

The taxi approaches from Saxmundham, bringing the first

of my guests. The car pulls over into the dry track opposite the cottage, and Nelson gets out. His long Madchester locks have been cut short. I show him into the cottage and through into the lounge. He sits on the sofa.

'Would you like some tea or coffee?' I ask from the kitchen. 'Perhaps opium tea? Is it too early for opium tea?'

He settles for Nescafe.

'How are things?' I ask.

'I'm still at the pub. Nothing new happening on the job front. You?'

'I'm a different person now.'

He looks askance.

'I've got a new name.' I pronounce it for him – De-A-bay-tua – and relate its history and my ostensible motivation: the restoration of the patriarchal line.

'Nice one,' he says. 'You don't seem too bad.'

'What do you mean?'

'I didn't know what to expect. After your letters.'

'What letters?'

He shifts awkwardly on the sofa.

'The things you wrote about Sizewell…' His eyes crease with scrutiny and questioning. I must have written something else in the letters, something I have forgotten. I enjoy his mystification because I know that in my heart I am entirely sane and in control. I have chosen this, it has not been thrust upon me.

I say, 'We should walk to Sizewell, and take the Sizewell cure.'

Nelson's gaze is veiled with rustic scepticism, an expression considerably older than he is.

On the way out, we pass Will's office. Seventies flock wall paper covered in Post-it notes, various thoughts at rest like birds upon a branch, a hiatus in their long migration to the page.

'What's he like to work with then, this writer? After reading your letters, I thought he might be a bit of a fuckin' head-the-ball.'

'I am to familiarise myself with his oeuvre and its diaspora.'

Nelson shakes his head at the rare words and chuckles to himself.

I continue, 'By which I mean novels and short stories, then the journalism and cartoons. I am reading all of it. And the unpublished bits and bobs: the treatments, proposals, abandoned drafts. There's not a great deal of unpublished work. A couple of abandoned chapters on a non-fiction project called Junk Male.' I show Nelson the rest of the library. 'This is the drugs shelf, from *Smart Drugs* to Thomas Szasz's arguments for legalisation. This is the literary biography shelf – William Burroughs, Hunter S Thompson. Here is what we are reading at the moment: Bruce Wagner, Dennis Cooper, Tobias Woolf. Here are the core fictional influences: Lem's *Solaris*, Swift, Ballard, Kafka, Céline, you'll recognise *On the Road*, and so on.'

I walk over to the fireplace. Balanced on its mantel are works of reference, the two-volume edition of the *Oxford English Dictionary* and the well-thumbed thesaurus.

'A thesaurus is a vital instrument in the writer's armoury,' I quote.

'He's clever then?'

'I'm learning about psychiatry, anthropology, the different character of north London suburbs. Even after four years of university, I've barely scratched the surface of what I need to know. I'm discovering how limited our upbringing was.'

We leave the cottage and walk up the rising, high-hedged Church Lane, then turn toward the village.

'I'm learning a lot about class too. Did you know that rich people have their own bank? It's called Coutts. It's not on the high street. He taught me about anti-Semitism too. He's very sensitive to it. Did you know that some of the upper classes hate Jews?'

'We get National Front in the pub. They sit in the corner. Skinheads organising, plotting. Dickheads.'

'Growing up in Maghull, we learned nothing. *Nothing*. Because everyone was the same as us.'

The houses in Knodishall are from the same 1960s stock as the houses in Maghull. We stop in the local pub for a pint. It's empty and unweathered by custom, the atmosphere is stilted, like drinking in a neighbour's living room. The barman seems nervous, and confers with the landlady.

'Do they seem weird to you?' Nelson asks, returning with a pair of pints.

'They're not used to customers,' I reply. 'Do you see the bar? The bar is made of a wood-effect vinyl over MDF chipboard, the bottles in the optics are all precisely a quarter-full, and the chalkboard next to the dartboard is entirely black. It's never been used.'

'Is it always like this?' whispers Nelson.

'I don't know. Will and I never dared come in here before. We tend to skirt around the village.'

'Never dared?'

'Because of the opium. Opium has always been cultivated in Suffolk. The Victorian pharmacists relied upon it. Today, on the quiet, farmers grow opium to supply morphine for the NHS. Some of it goes missing.'

Nelson looks again at the ad hoc furnishings with a barman's expert eye.

'None of this furniture looks used.'

'No, I suppose it wouldn't be.'

'What do you mean?'

I lean over and whisper, 'It doesn't feel right, does it?'

He finishes his pint.

'Shall we push on?'

The water tower marks the outskirts of Leiston. A quiet Wednesday afternoon in the town. Half-day closing. We've arrived too late for lunch. We don't know what the rules are. That feeling of unbelonging is familiar to both of us. We are both a long way from home and are never going back but the etiquette of these new places in which we find ourselves is obscure.

After failing to buy a sandwich, we decide to regroup in the White Horse. We know how pubs work.

Nelson asks, 'Do you remember the holiday in Settle?'

The holiday in Settle. Five fifteen-year-old lads in all their pomp, acne and virginity, thirty-five cans of Australian lager a night and a handful of expensive cigars that took a week to smoke. The caravan steamed with sexual repression and intense sexual curiosity about girls, about each other. The odd torn page of pornography or softcore blue movie aside, our bodies were closely guarded secrets. Drunk, I ran around and around the campsite. Going nowhere. We went into town and followed girls at a safe distance. We broke into a paper factory, hopping over the wall and when the dogs started barking, I lost my nerve and fled across the dark fields. I was wearing a bright white coat and Nelson shone his torch on me as I tried to scuttle and crouch for cover. Finally, in desperation for something to mark the moment, we leapt from a high wall and into a foaming weir.

'Nothing happened on that holiday,' I say. 'There should have been a rite of passage.'

'We got pissed.'

'And nothing happened.'

'What did you want to happen?'

'Something meaningful. Memorable. Like in the films.'

Nelson chuckles to himself, 'Do you remember when you ordered a hug of tea in the café?'

'It was a handwritten menu,' I explain. 'The "M" looked like a "H" and I assumed that a hug of tea was a Yorkshire variation of the traditional mug of tea.'

He says, 'It's like you can't see what is obvious to everybody else.'

Nelson lights a Marlboro Red.

'I've missed this,' he says. 'Proper conversation. The thing about being a barman is that people are there to bore the fuck out of you.'

We talk about his pub in Oldham and its alcoholics, the regulars. The civil servants who drink at lunchtime and are full of their own importance. The middle-aged Man Utd fan who reminisces about the fights of his youth. The man who talks as if everyone in Oldham knows him, about the business he is building on the Isle of Man and the beautiful young wife he has at home.

'None of which is true,' says Nelson.

'Does it have to be true?'

'He's deluded.'

'People are made out of stories. The stories they tell themselves and the stories they tell other people.'

I had transcribed Will Self's interview with the author and psychoanalyst Adam Phillips, and this line about stories was my half-understood rendering of Phillips' thought. To my associative way of thinking, the notion of a self made out of stories was congruent to the sympathetic magic of the Aboriginal witch doctors, their manipulation of symbols to alter people and events. The power of language, the shaping force of a narrative. Not that I had ever dared speak in that way myself. That is, truthfully. I was in the habit of lying because

I was more interested in the fictions of myself than the facts. *You can't see what is obvious to everybody else.* In the cottage, far away from my past, I have been free to elaborate myself. The boy I was in the caravan in Settle is gone, forgotten.

'There is a Lancaster lass at the pub,' he says. 'Karen. She has a plait all the way down her back and is full of her own importance. Called me *the quiet one.* The landlady found me in the cellar room, giving her head on the edge of a keg.' His voice is deep with cigarettes. 'I'm a shy boy, really,' he says, pleased with himself. 'But since the incident, I've acquired a bit of a reputation with the ladies.'

'So the job has been good to you.'

He ponders his condition, then exhales.

'My life is a mess. It's been a hot summer. I can't open my bedroom window because of the alarms. The TV permanently fucking on as usual. The murmur of the cellar coolers, always fucking going. There's a bus terminal outside. I watch the buses come and go. Orange and white, they are. After my shift, I'm trapped there. Where else am I going to go: to another pub?'

I listen but do not offer reassurance. I am trying to weigh it up in my mind: the benefits of promiscuity against the deficits of dead-end work.

Nelson taps out his cigarette. 'One good thing. The hot weather broke in a storm. I watched it through my bedroom window. It lit up the night. It was a beautiful electrical storm, you know. Sexy weather.'

It is late in the afternoon, too late perhaps for the Sizewell cure. But we can't go home yet. Nothing has happened. We walk out of Leiston on King George's road, past Lover's Lane, then on toward Sizewell gap. I find a footpath across the fields. The sky is darkening. It's not quite mushroom season, and it is far too late in the day to pick them; nonetheless I prance around the cowpats in search of the wavy stems and sticky brown transparent nipple-peak of the liberty cap mushroom. I find plenty of likely-looking fungi. But I cannot be certain they will be hallucinogenic and not lethally poisonous. Feeling the need for something stronger, for something to bring on the rest of the night, I lead Nelson down to the empty house in the lee of Sizewell. I position him in the garden so that he can listen to the thrum of the reactors and marvel at the suburban blasphemy of being able to gaze at a nuclear facility from the comfort of one's own yard. The power lines overhead are frankly conspiratorial.

We stand as the dusk steadily advances. Summer has gone. The reckoning is upon us. The fields are in sore need of a scarecrow. The crows help themselves. The garden is dark and Nelson's face is obscure. I crouch to inspect the wet hollows, turning back the long grass in case there are mushrooms in the shadows.

'What will happen to us, do you think?' He sounds worried. 'Is this who we are going to be?'

'Who knows what will happen?'

We go to another pub. The Vulcan Arms is at the end of the road leading into the nuclear complex. The air of conspiracy between the barman and his two regulars is thick. It's my round. As the barman pours my beers, the regulars resort to a pre-prepared conversation, the hairs on the back of their hands prickling at my presence.

'Did you see the news about the bank manager who was killed?'

'Yes.'

'I knew it was the husband.'

'So they said.'

I take my drinks and return to the table. The regulars stop talking and only resume when Nelson or I venture to the toilet or back to the bar.

'*This place,*' whispers Nelson.

'They clearly know about us,' I reply. 'Security will have observed our approach. The house that I took you to marks the outer perimeter of their surveillance. The nuclear industry has had trouble with protestors. The nuclear waste leaves here by train and then goes through North London, past Acton and then beyond to be reprocessed. They take it out on flatbed trucks, in a big concrete crate with fluted winged sides, to cool it down. Whenever the level crossing is down, then you know that the waste is being shipped out.'

'It's a secret?'

'National security secret. All you'd have to do is find the right vantage point in London, perhaps someone's garden backing onto the North London railway line, and fire a rocket launcher at the crate as it goes by. You could render Hampstead uninhabitable for ten generations.'

Nelson lights a cigarette.

'A hug of tea,' he laughs.

'*Mug* looked like *hug*; it was her handwriting.'

'No-one else would have looked at the menu and thought, oh, they must have invented a new term for "mug of tea". You were a very awkward lad.'

'What do you mean?' Seemingly amused but quite defensive.

'You weren't very popular. Certainly not with the girls. Who would've known that you'd grow up like this?'

On the windy beach, I try to gather firewood to make a fire for us. But I can't find any. Night has fallen too fast. The silhouette of the pumping inlet out in the cold waters. Had I hoped that we would swim out there together? Too drunk now. Wasted on every level. Holding a branch in one hand, and a Zippo lighter in the other, stumbling around on the steep pebbled shore. I can't make it happen. I can't get the fire started. Or rather, it has already burned out. I've come back here because this was where it happened, where I became somebody else, but I don't have the words to make it happen again. The year has moved on. The beach is colder and darker than I remember.

Nelson returns to the Vulcan Arms and calls us a cab. Back in the cottage, after a few more honks on the special cigarette, I resolve that I will finish off the opium. In the kitchen, I make a big hug of opium tea.

The bin bags containing Will's old existence have been unpacked and restored to life. Under the sink, the bag of opium heads rots and seethes with new insect life. Throughout the cottage, dissolution is accompanied by processes of growth and transformation.

The cottage is a tomb. The cottage is a womb. We are living on the edge of the middle of nowhere. We are liminal, in the flux of opposing processes, creation and destruction, husking off an old self and flexing the taut wet-born sheen of a new one. Neither this nor that, yet both.

I take another volume of anthropology off the shelf. Will Self has been reading Lévi-Strauss, I am reading Mary Douglas. JG Frazer's *The Golden Bough* is close at hand. The deep patterns of human society are at work in the cottage; the rite of passage, consciously and unconsciously enacted, with Will as mentor and I as the neophyte. As the elder, his authority is absolute. He embodies the axiomatic values of a society.

But which society?

Not the society of John Major's Britain, that's for sure. The previous year, Major set out his vision of the future for Britain: 'a country of long shadows on county grounds, warm beer, invincible green suburbs, dog lovers and pools fillers and – as

George Orwell said – "old maids bicycling to Holy Communion through the morning mist".' Not Maghull, then. Maghull was the country of geography teachers in the bookies and teenagers under the canal bridge mixing Thunderbirds with paracetamol. A land of cold lager, new estates, cabbage fields and a large asylum. Of socialist history teachers cycling to lessons where they spent two years instructing their pupils in the Russian Revolution but never getting around to Stalin.

And then there is Will Self Country. On field trips to London, Will has taken me on brief tours of the streets tagged with his memories; a place where dead mothers live on in North London suburbs, a place where sons skulk around inner city car parks scoring drugs; a country of stained concrete anomie, the commuters trudge from high rise via concrete island to work in the offices of the grey area. Windows down, Nirvana on the stereo again, the Citroën DSV elbows its way down Greek Street. He instructs me: Bar Italia, 'this is where you get your coffee', a corner restaurant in Chinatown, 'this is where you eat', the Groucho Club, 'this is where you drink'. Here, the body is the territory. Tunnels concentrate dreams. We stand at the back of a crowded tube train, head and shoulders above the other Londoners. The doors open and more bodies pour in to the train. 'My god,' says Will, 'it's an unstaunchable wound of *people*.' The train stops at Oxford Circus, and we ascend to find ourselves once again on Sizewell shore. Kick away the shingle and expose a hairy patch of Gulliver's belly. The Lilliputians have encased his head within the geodesic helmet of Sizewell B.

According to the anthropological texts, liminality is a stage of reflection. It is the sacred realm of primitive hypothesis. Neophytes are 'alternately forced and encouraged to think about their society, their cosmos, and the powers that generate and sustain them.' In the cottage, received ideas are broken down into their constituents under the intense rays of scrutiny, sarcasm and reverie. By exaggerating components of the everyday, by distorting the scale of common objects or the body itself, commonplace ideas are made into objects of reflection. Our work in the cottage is to render England strange so that we may study it, and by doing so, return from the liminal state transformed. Then we will be ready to assume our position in society. William James notes that during the liminal process, monsters may be deployed to startle neophytes into thinking about objects, persons, relationships, and features of their environment they have hitherto taken for granted.

In the dew-wet garden, Nelson and I huddle under respective blankets. The star field is deep. Wispy nebula spirals spin under the influence of opium tea. I walk around the garden until the gut ache gets too much. Back under the blanket, I find myself in the graveyard of St Andrews Church, in Maghull. If we were a religious family, then St Andrews would be our family church. From its pulpit, I gave the Christmas readings as head boy. On its pews, I sat through the funeral of my grandmother; she was unexpectedly light in her coffin, the pallbearers stumbled and almost dropped her. My father-in-law's funeral will also be here, and I will stand next to the pulpit with his grandchildren and read out their memories of him. My mother's funeral will take place here, and I will write and read the eulogy. That's a long way in the future. My sister will also be married in St Andrews Church. The congregation files outside the church and awaits the emergence of the new bride. In the church gardens, next to the church cemetery, past and future are intermingled. This is a wedding that is also a funeral. Life and death. Opposing processes, to begin with, though over time, opposites tend to transform themselves into one another. Neither this nor that yet both. The congregation weeps throughout the vows. We all take turns to reminisce about the virtues and deeds of the bride and groom. The pallbearers carry the bride back up the aisle. My relatives are there. People I barely know. The bride turns and to the delight of the bridesmaids throws a skull into the air for them to catch. The hearse arrives to take them to their honeymoon. The guests form a guard of honour. As the bride passes through the arch, we throw confetti into the air and it comes down as ash, crematorium ash which leopards then tigers her white dress.

The next morning, Nelson and I are in the garden when El arrives at the cottage, a paisley-patterned travel bag swinging from her hand. Nelson sits in a deckchair, watching the breeze clean the ash from the end of his cigarette. I am carrying the rifle and have lined up some empty half-bottles of whisky on the wall for target practice.

'What have you two been up to?' she says.

I shrug. She kisses me hello. I have been on my own for so long that her touch shocks me. Her hands warm on my back, the scented grain of her foundation, the warmth of her neck against the cold tip of my nose. She drops her bag off in my bedroom, gets changed and then we take a taxi to Aldeburgh, leaving Nelson, who seems subdued after the previous evening's excesses, to his own devices in the cottage.

The cab drops us at the fishermen's huts on the front. A seaside town out of season. Fishing skiffs hoisted high up the beach, their rigging pealing in the stiff sea wind. In the dining room of an empty hotel, we sit in winged-back chairs and drink lukewarm coffee and eat scones served on paper doilies. Through a leaded window, the sea toils grey and white. In the window box, there are peonies and dead pansies. From a silver-plated tin, I pinch out some tobacco and make a roll-up, filling the time with smoke.

After coffee, I take El by the hand. We walk toward the sea, and stumble down an embankment of shingle together.

'It's been a while,' I say.

'This is the longest we've been apart. How do I look?' She gives me a twirl. She's wearing a tartan-checked pinafore dress over a cream long-sleeved shirt with dark tights and maroon Doc Marten boots. She is a foot shorter than I am and this gives me licence to get lost in my own thoughts until she brings me back down to earth.

'You look like I hoped you would,' I say.

The waves break noisily against the pebbled shoreline, and then withdraw, hissing loudly. A woman in a white swimming cap walks steadily into the sea and then floats serenely out on the current.

'More,' demands El. She tilts her head back so that her blonde hair is suffused with the reflection of the low sun.

'You look like you are enjoying my gaze.'

'I do enjoy being looked at by you,' she says, raising her left foot to point at me.

We kiss and lie down together in the pebbles.

'Then let me look at you.' I lie alongside her and peer along her profile.

'Is it good?' she asks.

I get up and walk around her smile. 'From this angle, it's all good.' I crouch down behind her head, and touch her warm scalp, pinkly visible through the crown of her hair. El's hair contains variations upon the theme of blonde. These variegated strands recall the ploughed lines in the fields around the cottage.

'I like you close-up,' I say.

'Better than far away?'

I take a few steps back. El, propped on her elbows, gazes out to sea. The white cap of the swimmer rises and falls with the incoming tide.

'Far away has the advantage of a sea setting.'

'Does the sea flatter me or do I flatter the sea?'

'You can do without it.'

'Overall, then, how would you say I looked? Different than you remember?'

'Colder.' I hand her my long black coat which she winds around herself until only her head is visible. This image disturbs me. It is like she is wrapped in a shroud. An echo of the opium vision of St Andrews church. The wedding that was also a funeral.

'Let me in,' I say.

She flaps one wing of the coat aside and I lie upon her and kiss her forehead.

'One last time,' says El. 'Tell me how I look?'

The swimmer comes out of the water. She wades through the wash with a towel slung over her shoulder. The rest of the beach is deserted and, either because she does not see us lying there or perhaps because she has outgrown shyness, the woman pulls her bathing costume off, exposing her white, fleshy breasts.

'Do you see her?' I say to El. 'She must be fifty, fifty-five years old. She has an image in her mind of how beautiful she was when she was twenty-four.' I kiss El again. 'That's what you look like: you are the memory of what it was like to be young.'

I help her up. We walk further along the beach, past a Martello tower, and toward the distant secret masts of Orford Ness, separated from the mainland by a narrow channel and the source of some paranoid speculation back at the cottage. What are they doing out on the Ness, we wonder? Is it a listening station or an early warning system from the Cold War? There are rumours of UFO sightings in the forest. There is no way of knowing the truth – this is pre-internet – and so imagination fills in the gaps. That's what I miss the most, the gaps.

In the pub, El orders a pint of prawns and shows me how to shell these strange sea insects. She asks for some tartare sauce with her new potatoes and the waitress refuses to bring it, insisting that tartare sauce should never be served with new potatoes. I am aghast at the complications entailed in social interaction.

The cheeseboard is a selection of Italian cheeses: hunks of mozzarella, parmesan and taleggio, delivered with simpering superiority.

El says, 'Don't these people know anything? You don't serve Italian cheese like *this*.'

We are poor people with sophisticated tastes. El slips the entire parmesan into a napkin and hands it under the table for me to place in the deep pocket of my black coat. Then she takes the taleggio.

'We'll have that for lunch tomorrow, in a salad,' she says. 'Serves them right.'

We return to the cottage at night. Tall candles flare in the front yard. With Nelson we sit around the fire drinking whisky and playing the Rizla game. I write 'Robin, nephew of Kermit' on her Rizla and stick it to her forehead. El guesses it first time, to the befuddlement of us all. Magical thinking. Nelson is quiet, he feels superfluous now that El is here. Something else too, I wonder if he came here hoping for some change within himself, some upturn in fortunes, and whatever was needed has not occurred, if it ever could, and so he must return to the pub in Oldham, to his bedroom with the locked windows and its limited view of the bus terminal.

I take El to bed and we have uninhibited noisy sex, the kind of sex which builds up into a relentless momentum, a rolling overpowering process which I am both driving forward and being carried upon.

In the next morning, Nelson slips away without saying goodbye. Later, I will hear from mutual friends that he seemed shaken by his time in the cottage and found the whole experience disturbing. Of the content of my letters, he said only that I wrote to him about a birdman.

IDLERS

Bret Easton Ellis said that the aspiring writer must get a hundred thousand words out of the way first. A hundred thousand unpaid speculative words before the acolyte can expect to write something worth reading. Journalism doesn't count. Nor does the drafting and redrafting of acceptance speeches for imaginary award ceremonies. A hundred thousand words of fiction, and then begin in earnest.

Writing a novel requires such patience and stamina. A notable few claimed to have dashed through it – Faulkner's *As I Lay Dying*, Kerouac's *On the Road*. Unlike poets, who can spend a lifetime dining out on one good hour, novelists must solve the logistics of the long haul, and that takes planning, research and stealth. This workload can make the novelist managerial and distracted, never really there because they are concerned with the elsewhere of their fiction. In terms of the number of hours clocked up in a seat, the novelist is the long-distance lorry driver of literature.

Ambition, overleaping itself, gets in the way of such sedentary virtues. As a young man, I could barely write a paragraph without wondering: am I James Joyce yet? Lou Reed sang, you can't be Shakespeare, you can't be Joyce, so what is left instead? Lou Reed! None of us are going to be Lou Reed. We're not even going to be Sterling Morrison or Moe Tucker. There comes a time when a young man must admit to himself that he will never play the Bard. That he will never be *Heat* magazine's Torso of the Week.

I know the pains of ambition; the dry-mouthed anxiety in the presence of opportunity, a sharp yank of regret, every morning, that you are not the person you hoped to be. Nursing a half-written first novel in the desk drawer is like suffering a debilitating, incurable but minor medical condition. Friends come over. They don't really want to talk about your diseased ambition again. But drunk and adamant, you produce the manuscript from a desk drawer and insist that they read a bit of it.

You search their faces for the first signs of rapture.

They stop, and point to a word, saying 'I'm sure it's not spelt "metasised", it's "metastasised".' Or some such minor error. Writing is the only treatment for the sickness of being unread but it's not a guaranteed cure.

Sometimes friends say to me, 'Oh I hope you never write about me in your stories.'

I write about them all the time. You can always rely on your friends not to read your stuff.

The egotism that propels aspiring writers also holds them back. The ego is threatened by the truth, and first drafts are hard truths in black-and-white. Publication is not the end of it.

At some point, you are going to make a mistake. A good writer will play whack-a-mole with their narcissism, hammering away at measly grievances and power fantasies whenever they pop up, suppressing personal ambition in a broader ambition for the work.

For the majority of writers, the most they can hope for is to write something good which stays good all the way through and remains good every time they look at it, month after month, year after year. But it's hard to stay humble when ambition burns like an evil star.

How does the writer learn the art of distinguishing between useful and self-torturing ambition? How do you get humble? By writing books that don't make money. By writing the books that get amazing reviews and that no-one buys. By writing the books that no-one reviews and that no-one buys. By writing the novel that wins awards and is an experience so dispiriting that you never want to write again. By being the author of a work of genius that is finally discovered after ten years in the wilderness and is published to wide acclaim and makes just enough money to replace the boiler.

Submitting a novel for consideration by publishers is like crawling alongside a conga line; a dancer occasionally pauses in their joy to stick out a velvet-slippered foot and deliver an adroit kick to your gut then on they dance and on you crawl.

As a vehicle for ambition, the novel is a fucking jalopy. The wheels come off before you are even out of the garage. If you want to earn the admiration of your peers and a steady income without the need for a steady job, then do not accept a lift from the fucking novel. If you seek self-doubt, the indifference of your peers, long hours of unpaid labour behind the wheel then, by all means, climb on board.

I mean, look at the state of that writer! On the shortlist for the

Booker Prize back in the day, but now they shuffle around town, jowly, in sweatpants and cheap black trainers, a few possessions in an oft-used plastic bag. Instead of those adverts on daytime TV asking for donations to support a homeless dog or goat, there should be adverts for the Home For Unwanted Authors, presented by Alan Yentob or some figurehead of the arts. Watch the advert, here comes Yentob, outside the kennels, patting the heads of impoverished refugees from the midlist. Calling in at the content paddock where authors are forced to prance around and around in circles for the edification of social media.

Yentob turns to camera: 'As little as a pound a day could help a writer resole their shoes, or put new tyres on their old car. And if you cannot send money, then at least send some alcohol. And if you cannot send alcohol, then at least send food. Or children's shoes.'

This desperate state of affairs was not the case in the Nineties. Back then, even supermodels would write novels to improve their profile.

* * *

In 'A Short History of the English Novel', from Will Self's collection *Grey Area*, literary ambition seethes behind the servitude of London's waiters. A publisher, Gerard, and his female acquaintance wander through a lunchtime in Soho and Covent Garden, through Bar Italia, Joe Allen, and Wheeler's of Old Compton Street. At each establishment, they encounter waiters who are also aspiring writers – they are separated from their ambition by a vowel and a consonant. Each waiter in turn pitches their prospective novel to Gerard and his acquaintance, our narrator. These novels include a reimagining of *Fanny Hill* from the point of view of the dog of Eric Gill, the arts and crafts artist who experimented sexually with his dog and discovered that, if properly prompted, 'a dog will join with a man'. Then, in Bar Italia, Gerard and the narrator listen to a waitress recount her near-future novel concerning a town surrounded by health facilities, an institutional doughnut which acts as a 'means of filtering out undesirables who want to enter the town and controlling those who already live in it'. Each putative novel is a recognisably Selfian conceit, the kind of riffs that he improvises at will when in the mood, and which can turn easily from comic inversion to bleak diagnosis of the prevailing condition.

Toward the end of the 'A Short History of the English Novel', a grandee of publishing requests his bill 'using that universal hand signal of squiggling with an imaginary pen on the sheet of the air'. The signature causes outrage in the waiting staff. The signing of contracts to write books, the signing of books the writer has written – it is the mark of authenticity which divides the published author from the aspirant. Once, Will did toy with the idea of getting me to sign books for him when, after an event, a back room full of novels awaited his signature and he had a pressing appointment with fun. I had already taught myself his signature and his characteristic sign-off of 'Hell and High Water' to deal with cheques and minor correspondence in absentia. In the end, he dallied with the possibility for ten seconds or so and then resolved to sign the books himself. He would not betray this covenant of authenticity. He would never betray the ideal of literature.

By comparing the mark of the author to the air signature of the Soho restaurant, the story admits to literary idealism and, in the next breath, shows us the source of its corruption. The English novel is scorned as part of the service industry. Gerard's job in publishing is something that is neither editorial nor high-profile. He talks of books 'as so many units, trafficked hither and thither as if they were boxes of washing powder.' He reduces authors 'to the status of assembly line workers, trampish little automata who were merely bolting the next lump of text on to an endlessly unrolling narrative product.' The casual hauteur of a diner settling a large bill they can easily afford is conflated with the largesse of a publisher, putting their mark on a contract with a writer, signing a cheque for a large advance and exercising *droits du seigneur* to commercialise the seething ambition of a highly-strung aspirant.

Gerard blasphemes against literature. Literature is the transcendental signifier that gives meaning to the suffering of the writer, transmutes experience into art, forgives all sins. Literature is a moral good; the generation of writers thriving in the Nineties were the last generation who could seriously entertain the prospect of posterity, that secular lie of eternal life.

A lifelong faith in literature must be defended. When Nick Hornby wrote in the *Modern Review* of the impossibility of writing a novel, Will seethed. 'Hornby dissed the novel.' It was the only time we ever riffed about violence. That if we were to see Hornby in the Groucho Club we might rough Hornby up, Self and I. As it was, Hornby would write his novel, and Will would hustle that novel – *High Fidelity* – into the corner of the *Modern Review* and knee it in the groin.

It is not the commercial aspect of publishing that is critiqued in 'A Short History of the English Novel'. That would be redundant. Rather Gerard exemplifies a trend particular to the Nineties: the emergence of nebulous roles within creative industries (an oxymoron that seemed amusing at the time, less so in an age in which writers are commissioned by algorithm) staffed by people who adopt managerial argot so that they are regarded by their masters as capitalist realists and not the ne'er-do-well, vaguely leftie arts graduates they once were.

I started work at 1 Hall Cottages on the 20th of July. Tony Blair was elected leader of the Labour opposition party the following day. His New Labour project was inspired by the methods of Bill Clinton's campaign team, specifically Dick Morris' notion of triangulation. In triangulation, you occupy the ideological ground of the enemy. If your rivals are tough on crime, then you are tougher. If your enemy cuts taxes, you cut taxes. For a left-wing party to gain power over an electorate shaped by right-wing, free market ideology, New Labour believed they had to imitate the opposition. Triangulation was the mask that became the face.

At the end of 'A Short History of the English Novel', the narrator is revealed to be a waiter called Geraldine who works at Le Caprice (a real restaurant, although the name is aesthetically pertinent). Her maître d', Marcel, chides Geraldine for her lateness and she resumes her duties without rancour. She is the feminine counterpart to Gerard, both waiter and writer of the story we are reading. Gerard and Geraldine, two aspects of a self. The one who sells and the one who serves. The doubling of the self caused by triangulation. This is a short history of the English novel, and this is how it ends: with a covert faith in the transcendence of literature and the recognition that ambition and commercial nous are required in the service of that faith.

In the culture, the writer has been elevated into a heroic figure of non-compliance. Living after the total victory of capitalism, in which the future promises only further indignity, it is natural that a beset middle class should hold up the path of the writer as a viable escape route. The writer mines memory and imagination, refining raw material of the self into the commodity of the novel. The alluring myth of the novel is that it monetises the self without compromising or subduing it. On the contrary. It externalises and memorialises the self. In an article on the allure of literary biography, Will Self notes that 'The writer, in an age of mass standardisation, corporatism, stereotypy, and the remorseless eradication of any meaningful individuality…represents the promise of an untrammelled life.'

The *promise*. The experience of being a writer does not live up to this fantasy. If power and wealth can only be obtained by imitating the mode of the enemy, then self-hatred is part of that deal. Triangulation chokes off oxygen to the imagination.

Filing away Will's paperwork, I come across a sheaf of business cards printed up with his name and number. They bear the legend: 'Will Self: 24-Hour Emergency Writer'. Ambition. Hustle. Accept all commissions. Always deliver and always get paid. Play up the vivid public persona and use it to smuggle the work into the culture. The side effect of such a public persona is that it becomes the object of other people's frustrated ambition, and they take out their grievances upon the work. The plan had been to circulate the cards at the Groucho Club and in phone boxes across Soho but I think, in the end, he decided not to. The joke was thin, and, behind it, the malformed silhouette of ambition could be discerned. A writer, once successful, must let go of the grievances built up during apprenticeship.

* * *

The *Idler* party is at 55 Turnmill Street, next to Farringdon station, in a part of London that estate agents will later encourage journalists to call Clerkenwell. During the night, Farringdon is largely uninhabited. The offices erected in the late Eighties property boom are empty. On Fleet Street, a pigeon's foot traps a double page spread from the *Evening Standard*. Unemployment is falling. Norman Lamont's long-mocked green shoots of recovery have arrived. The economy is on the up. The tides of capital that withdrew from London during the recession are slowly trickling back. Bright young things come to Farringdon for early morning beers, bacon butties outside Smithfield Meat Market, and to join the shirtless punters spilling out of Trade nightclub at Turnmills. Thus, London renews its complexion with young blood.

Follow the brick wall that runs the length of Turnmill Street until you find a door, go in, then walk down a steep dark staircase, past a shabby room and a rotten office, down more creaking stairs into a central hall where an ad hoc bar is serving bottled beer and cans of lager from bins of ice. The party is in its throes, a hundred or so people. Stepladders have been provided so that the party goers can move from one part of the complex to the next. The toilet is a broken cistern with a yabbering flush. Climb the stepladder out of the dance floor and you will be surprised to find yourself outside again, on a shadow lane, set well below Turnmill Street.

Standing in the secret lane, smoking Silk Cut and chatting, is Tom Hodgkinson, the editor of the *Idler*. The handsome effect of his dark corona of Byronic curls is undone by the two pronounced fangs that push ahead of his front teeth. I've met him before, briefly, at one of Will Self's book launches in a member's club where, in a back room, Julie Burchill sat in an armchair with young men kneeling at her feet. Tom is far more welcoming. He has the bulging eyes of an enthusiast and the instincts of a hack, two urgencies held in abeyance by his cultivated laziness. These contrary impulses determine his editorial style. He flies on the serendipity of social encounters. He is interested in the underground, skateboarding and Rough Trade, the rock gods on welfare and the bohemians who blow it all.

Next to Tom is Gavin Pretor-Pinney, blonde and more

conventionally handsome, with a rustic blush on his cheeks. He is the designer of the *Idler*, and it is his attention to detail and strong visual aesthetic, applying Occam's Razor to every layout, that elevates the soft-headed *Idler* above other counter-cultural zines, with their wonky close-set text and dated punk look.

Pleasantries out of the way, I pitch articles. But there are a hundred other people in the room who want the ear of the Idlers: photographers and artists and other journalists, young and old. I'm still learning my metropolitan manners: fill your allotted span and do not attempt to prolong it, air-kiss left and right with women and men, and ease off on the handshakes. The meercatting, that tendency to peer over the shoulder of the person you are talking to, trying to ascertain if a more important conversation is happening elsewhere, is particularly disconcerting. I came of age around pub tables, in solid stable drinking sessions with people who had committed to the evening: in other words, a captive audience. The fluidity of these gatherings makes me queasy with self-doubt.

At the *Idler* party, it's not all media types. There are various people attached to the venue: sculptors who are also blacksmiths, a Tibetan prince in exile, numerous DJs who all work in media sales (in the Nineties, I am forever having my ear chewed by some narcotically-charged salesman carrying a box of records). Here is Tintin, the Vietnamese chef in a tweed suit, who tells me a long story of his own devising (but it is basically Oedipus), and here is the drug dealer who also works for BT. A bit of this and a bit of that. The party is an arty soup of duckers-and-divers with Oxbridge croutons.

Tom introduces me to people as Will Self's assistant, and this is enough to attract a *moue* of interest. I am a nobody who works for somebody. I talk to Heather, who works at *Harpers*

& Queen.

'Your roll-ups,' says Heather. 'Could I have one?'

I make her the mundane cigarette.

'My father used to smoke these,' she says. 'They remind me of him.'

I flick through the *Idler* until I rest, ostentatiously, upon my article and my by-line. There is a photograph of me in the mist, gazing off at the pylons on the flat plain. It is the realisation of my dream. More than I could ever have hoped for. Publication is a fleeting high.

'So you work for Will Self,' says Heather. 'What's he like?'

'He's very generous. My first night I arrived there was no bed for me, and so he offered me his, while he drove off to London.'

'You're his assistant.'

'Amanuensis.'

I don't know how to prolong the conversation. Then I remember that in these situations, the ones involving *people*, it is customary to inquire about the life of the other person. Turns out that Heather runs the front section of *Harpers & Queen* and she is looking for a book reviewer.

'I review books,' I say, bringing the conversation back to me. It is not entirely untrue. I had been commissioned to write the book review round-up for the *Modern Review*, and this would have been my first big publication had the magazine not gone down before my work could see print, thereby establishing a recurring pattern in my career.

A rollie requires more drag than a straight smoke. I relight Heather's cigarette twice, three times for her before the novelty wears off. She takes out a Marlboro Light and moves on.

Left alone, I flick through the new issue of the *Idler*. Fat Freddy's Cat is on the cover, trailing an interview with Gilbert Shelton about the Freak Brothers and the Sixties underground.

The covers of previous *Idlers* reveal a restless quest for a counter-cultural identity particular to this new generation, Generation X. The first cover of the *Idler* featured Dr Johnson, and the magazine's stated aim is to update Johnson's eighteenth-century salon for the Nineties. The second issue carries Homer Simpson on the cover, the third issue a photograph of a pigeon. A pigeon! Commercial suicide. Kurt Cobain is on the cover of issue four. Blown away! Commercial genius. Thanks Kurt. The print run sells out. For issue five, the cover has a skateboarder and the promise of a slack summer. Issue six it's Audrey Hepburn as Holly Golightly presiding over a Cocktail Nation. The Easy Listening revival, a brief rummage around in kitsch for some dressing-up. The *Idler* is a quest for a usable past, each issue nostalgic for a time we never knew. Then Fat Freddy's Cat for issue seven – the Nineties as the upside-down version of the Sixties. Corinne Day's breakthrough photographs of Kate Moss in the *Face* and the promised third summer of love were published in the first blush of the Nineties. The spectre of the Sixties hangs around all the way up to the millennial feast. But what happens to us will not be a recapitulation of the Sixties. It will be a triangulation.

'We have new offices,' says Gavin. 'On Farringdon Road. The *Guardian* are letting us use some desks there for free.'

'Really?'

'Nothing official, just to see what happens,' he says. 'When I worked on the *Modern Review*, we used newspaper offices sometimes too. Not that they knew about it. You should pop by next time you are in London.'

I will, of course, I will.

I sit down on a wooden bench set on a rough concrete floor and drink quickly. The man next to me is a DJ, who hums and harrs when I ask about his day job (media sales). His gangly, ravey tattooed girlfriend opens beer bottles with her molars. She does 'the visuals' for his set. She keeps them on CD-ROM.

'What is this place?' I ask, gazing up at the brick arches. 'Some kind of warehouse?'

'It was full of wood when they found it.'

'Who?'

'George and Howard. It's part of their charity,' he says.

'What kind of charity?'

The music is too loud for him to bother explaining. He rocks his head from side to side, eyes closed. Ambition dictates I find someone else to speak to. I cannot waste the night. I must make further inroads, find leads, get off the bottom rung. 'These are the kind of people you should meet,' Will had said about the *Idler*. But my mother had offered more cautionary advice. 'Don't make the mistake of thinking you are like these people. You don't have their backup. Their *resources*.'

I follow Tom and Gavin upstairs. In a dusty side office, Howard and George are waiting. They run this place. Howard is part of a crew from a squatted street, Bavant Road in Camberwell, whose inhabitants are known as the Bavanti, and they are renovating the labyrinth. George's role is unclear. Tom thinks George might be the janitor. Negotiations are underway for the cost of the party.

'Shouldn't the venue be free?' I ask.

'We agreed a price, old boy,' says Howard, a squint in his right eye that grows excited at the prospect of negotiation.

I say, 'But you get all the take behind the bar.'

'Oh we'll have to watch this one,' says Howard to George.

'He's a *mickey mouser*,' says George, the oldest man in the room by fifteen years. Maybe more. George's hair is shaved into an upright brush. Behind his front teeth, he has two inches of molars missing on either side. His forearms are muscular from manual work.

'A sharp one,' says George.

'We'll watch this one,' agrees Howard. 'Next time, Tom, just send the Scouser to negotiate.'

'More of a challenge,' says George.

'What is this place?' I ask. 'It goes on forever.'

Howard rests his army boots on the drawer of a filing cabinet, in which there are rolls of thermal paper. The desks are covered in dust and tobacco. An incense stick burns next to a boarded-up window.

'This is our office.'

'The office for?'

'International Humanitarian and Aid Concern. IHAC. The parties help us to raise money for our work in Sarajevo.' The siege of Sarajevo is ongoing. Footage is released of what appear to be concentration camps on the news.

'Massacres happen when the international community cannot see what is going on,' says Howard. 'We're raising money to put in satellite modems and establish Sarajevo's first web server. There is a store and forward email network getting messages out of the siege of Sarajevo but the phone lines have been impacted by shelling.'

I had used JANET, the precursor to email and the World Wide Web, at university.

The origins of the Farringdon labyrinth are obscure. It has a massive walk-in safe, and we speculate that it was for once used for storage and workshops for the bullion brought in by train for Hatton Garden. When Howard took over the labyrinth, one of the old boys told him it was the place where the original strobe light was invented. It is owned by Railtrack who lease it to Howard and George for a peppercorn rent. Exactly why is unclear. When you are below street level, clarity is hard to come by. Certainly both men wish to cultivate mystique and to cloak the reality of who they are. When in his cups, George's monologues are endless plains across which the hapless listener wanders in search of full stops; they reveal nothing. Howard's smile is close to a wince, his speech peppered with deliberate archaisms – he calls me 'old boy' as if he were an avuncular major and not a squatter in paramilitary Camden market kit. Tom and Gavin, Howard and George. I've read a lot of books. But I can't read people. I take their proffered myths at face value, and proffer my own in turn.

Tom and Gavin return to the party. I stay behind with George and Howard. We are joined by Andy Sound Man. Andy Sound Man provides the sound system for every party. He is small, pale and perpetually wide-eyed: a Tommy in the Party Infantry.

'I'm going to take a party van to Sarajevo,' says Andy.

Howard chuckles.

'How are you going to break the siege of Sarajevo, Andy?' asks George.

Andy says, 'Howard can get me through the siege. We're going to put a satellite dish on top of the van and the Idlers will write articles and we'll broadcast them on the internet. We're going to deliver CDs to the pirate radio stations. We're going to take the party to the war.'

'A marvellous idea,' says Howard.

Andy shrugs. 'Why should they miss out on parties just because there's a war on?'

George cackles at this sentiment.

Andy adds, 'A bombed-out parliament would be a great place to have a party.'

In the Nineties, everywhere – from a system of sea caves to a transit van looping around the M25, from a ruined abbey on the Yorkshire Moors to a loading bay in Shoreditch – was a great place to have a party. And our social relations were conducted as if we were at a long party, always intoxicated, with nothing taken too seriously, and all unpleasantness put off until tomorrow.

Andy had stumbled on the vital truth about the Nineties: it may have been a soft-headed, heaving mass of meretricious triangulation but it was also a great place to have a party.

* * *

On the platform at Ipswich, a man speaks to me. He's unsteady and in his early fifties, wearing an old suit with his hair slicked back.

'Would you like a drink?' he asks.

'I'm waiting for my train.'

'Have a drink with me. I'll get you one.'

'I'll be OK.'

'I'm here if you need a drink.' He twists his fingers in the air in silent elaboration. 'The Great Redeemer, if you knowarramean. You'll see.'

He shakes his head slowly, and points with his cigarette at the long chestnut hair of a young woman buying coffee from the concession stand.

'A lovely lady. Is she yours?'

I demur.

'Do you know Rio?' He comes closer to confide in me. 'The statue of Virgin Mary? I sat up there with my lady and I could see, coming out of the ocean, the great wings of the manta ray, if you seewarramean. I said we could make love, but my lady said, make it out of what?'

The train arrives.

'Have a drink with me,' says the man. 'Then you'll see.'

I say no to him. I board the train, take a table seat in a tired and empty carriage. The man remains on the platform. Through the window, the lines of the land winnow and widen. Ravens on the wing, gliding alongside the train. I chew my fingernails and consider the man's peculiar remarks. The manta ray, breaking the surface of the water, leathery and sheathed with moisture, is a suppressed desire rising irresistibly to the fore. You forget so much. But not an unfulfilled desire or a frustrated ambition. They linger in the earth for decades.

GOOD

We drive to London in the Citroën. Somewhere on the A12, the exhaust rattles out of its bracket and drags along the road. Will pulls over onto the hard shoulder and we get out to inspect the damage, crouching to look at the underside of the car like we are experts. Will has an idea. He strides into the thicket and returns holding a tree branch. Then, in one swift movement, he whips off the belt of his trousers. He ties one end of the belt around the branch, and the other end around the exhaust; then to achieve the required tension, he wedges the branch into the boot of the car, and shuts the lid across the belt.

'Fixed,' he says.

The car stays fixed all the way into central London. It's a piece of good luck, the wind is at our backs. He drops me beside the A40, where the houses have been cleared in anticipation of an expansion of the road. I walk to El's house to pick her up for a night out.

El and I go to the French House in Soho for dinner with Will and Victoria. The upstairs dining room overlooks a neon-lit pornography store, where sad men come and go, servicing a peccadillo.

El is wearing a green shirt and black leggings. I am wearing one of Will's old blue suits, a hard-wearing tweed that has seen gutter action. It is 'virtually bullet-proof', he assures me, the gentleman's Kevlar.

The menu at the French House was typed up that morning and offers various neglected cuts of meat and offal, an emerging trend pioneered by the Hendersons running the kitchen. On the table, the tiny saucers of sea salt and ground black pepper are another new thing, signifiers of a change in taste. El and I joke about them but we share a quiet excitement for these tiny saucers: food and books are two ways in which we can get on in the world, accumulate cultural capital in lieu of financial capital; perhaps we will cook and write our way into a better life.

The table talk is of morality. From where do you derive your ideas of good or evil if you are not religious? The conversation arises from Will's projected novel 'Good'; goodness is what is on his mind, and therefore, what is on our mind too. Goodness is a subject for which El has more conviction than I can muster: a moral inclination only becomes a principle when you sacrifice something for it, and I have not made any sacrifices that I am aware of. I am not sure I have anything to sacrifice. Would my stereo count?

Will makes Soho happen for us. It is a burden of expectation for him, one that he throws off then takes up again in a way that is hard to anticipate. In Soho, it is difficult to tell self-destruction and self-advancement apart, sliding sideways along the bar rail, measuring out progress in cigarettes and sea breeze cocktails.

Masked ambition is the feeling I most associate with these evenings, moving from place to place in an entourage. Sometimes entourages will commingle, such as when we meet Damien Hirst's lot coming back from an opening or a bunch of reviewers, woozy from Bulgarian red, decamping from a launch. The art crowd are more naked in their ambition and more forceful in their enabling; once, after a long conversation with the photographer Rankin about fatherhood, I was approached by an ambitious couple who wanted to know exactly what Rankin had said to me, what was he interested in, what was my connection to him, and would I introduce them? 'I'm nobody,' I said, putting them out of their misery. They turned away from me.

Notoriety derives from the sabotaging of ambition, from refusing to conform to the way you are expected to behave to get on. Will told a story of his lunch with an editor or other bigwig; on the way to lunch, Will encountered a former acquaintance called Dave, who was down-at-heel, and brought him along; on arriving at the table of the bigwig, Will announced, 'They say there is no such thing as a free lunch. Well, there is for my friend Dave.' Sabotage prevents personal ambition from running amok. Ambition is a condiment not the meal, we take a pinch from the tiny bowl and sprinkle it over our work.

I try to take Will's convictions for my own but I cannot because they are a work in progress; the writing of each book changes the beliefs that form that book. Writing fiction is a way of rethinking who you are. It can leave you feeling unpicked as the writing of the book changes you.

How to be good in the world is not a question that interests me – and it would later be addressed directly in a Nick Hornby novel, *How To Be Good*. *Being good* implies a more authentic and cohesive sense of self than I can muster. I didn't get into fiction so that I could be held accountable for who I really am. I just want to know who I have to become next to succeed.

I turn the table talk back to writing. There is a morality in prose, I observe. I quote Maugham, from Cyril Connolly's *Enemies of Promise*: 'to write good prose is an affair of good manners.'

'We are aware of Cyril Connolly,' says Will, with mock grandeur. Cressida Connolly, the daughter of the renowned literary critic, is a friend. (Cyril Connolly's most famous line is that there is 'no more sombre enemy of good art than the pram in the hall.' For a while, I had two prams in my hall. Now my writing desk is actually in the hall. I am writing these words halfway between the shoe rack and the kids' bikes. What do you think of that, Cyril?)

The table cloth is paper and disposable. Will takes out his pen and draws on the cloth as we talk. He began his career as a cartoonist. On this London excursion, I've been retrieving copies of his illustrations and comic strips from the offices of the *New Statesman* in Shoreditch, adding them to his drawings in the archive, making a preliminary selection for inclusion in a collection of his journalism that – after some deliberation – will be titled *Junk Mail*. Its original title, the punning druggy 'Junk Male' has been junked, along with his proposed essays on drugs in collaboration with Dr Phil Robson. These essays were *meretricious*, he has decided, the word derived from *mereri* to be hired and *meretrix* or prostitute. The word confuses me because it is so close phonetically to *meritocracy* – 'a culture which rewards bright and ambitious people regardless of their origins' according to the OED.

Will draws a conga line of figures curling up one side of the tablecloth; my favourite of his cartoons is of an executive toy in which suspended ball bearings knock repetitively against one another; except, in the cartoon, the ball bearings are replaced by naked men and women, their clashing impacts expressing the impersonal contagion of desire. His cartoons show people on strings, people as glove puppets. This links with his disavowal of traditional characterisation in his fiction at this point, instead assuming an anthropological perspective on our society. There is always something or someone pulling the strings of desire. The group mind of 'The Quantity Theory of Insanity', his fictional theory that posits a limited amount of sanity in any social grouping, advances a lack of individual agency. His story 'The End of The Relationship' from *Grey Area* depicts an emotional Typhoid Mary spreading discord from couple to couple. The emotions we place within ourselves, as our most intimate creations, do not originate within us.

Will Self does not believe in traditional psychological realism in characterisation. His characters do not change in a progressive way. His characters violently metamorphose.

The starters arrive. El is talking about her idea of good, doing to others as you would have done to you, how religion extended our sphere of moral concern from families to strangers. Then she backs away from her own argument, not wanting to be seen to be religious. I'm aware that we are putting on a performance as a couple, helping one another to present the best version of ourselves.

We think we're on safer ground discussing *Pulp Fiction*, the script for which was sent to Will months ago. 'Because of the heroin scene,' he explains. El and I enjoyed *Pulp Fiction*. Will reckons it to be pseudo-hip drug pornography. But we have waltzed too far along the runway of enthusiasm for Tarantino to make our way back to the wings. The conversation runs aground. As with the retitling of Junk Male, Will wants to move beyond his early notoriety, the boring drug talk, the *meretricocracy.* There is an emerging awareness of responsibility in terms of drugs, a shift in emphasis away from sensation and intoxication.

We loop back to this question of the morality of style. From Connolly, Will has adopted the term 'mandarin' to describe an aspect of his own style. Citing De Quincey and his *Confessions of an English Opium Eater*, Connolly writes, 'The mandarin style at its best yields the richest and most complex expression of the English language.' At its worst, mandarin renders the written word as unlike as possible to the spoken one: 'It is the style of all those writers whose tendency it is to make their language convey more than they mean or more than they feel.'

The style of contemporaries like Martin Amis intermingles the demotic with the mandarin, a style that combines the rhythms and coinages of the colloquial with the aesthetic images and patterning of Nabokov. The resulting style is strongly voiced, intensely individual, entirely performative. Fine for the duration of a short story, whisper the entourage of reviewers, but can it be sustained for a novel; or, even, should it be sustained for a novel, doesn't the performance drown out the moral good of giving a voice to other people's lives?

The transparent style of George Orwell is used as riposte to mandarin prose. Cyril Connolly elides a passage of Orwell's transparent prose with a passage from the similarly see-through prose of Christopher Isherwood; this style is 'superlatively readable', Connolly argues, but renders the writers indistinguishable from one another; worse, 'these practitioners in the new vernacular' are swimming with the cultural tide, indistinguishable also from the general hackwork of copywriting, song lyrics and journalism. Connolly quotes Gide's dictum that a good writer should navigate *against* the current; as Will Self will later observe, Orwell's style makes him the nation's supreme mediocrity; it aspires to a construct of the general reader and their common sense that denies the polyphony and difference that keeps the English language vital.

'Style is not a manner of writing, it is a relationship; the relation in art between form and content,' declares Connolly. The progressive ideal in literary fiction is that the form is reinvented to express content. When the novel ceases to renew itself in this way, form becomes ossified, and the writer resorts to the conventions of realism and the kitsch of epiphanies, glancing emotions, authorial presence tastefully pared back. In Will Self's novels, puerility and puns run alongside vertiginous psychological reveries; druggy slurred pronunciations and grotesque body horror rubs up against philosophical inquiry. For about a month, he overuses the word 'gusset' in his conversation and articles, an invariably soiled gusset at that; the gusset bears the stamp of our embodiment, the fingerprint of the underself. The body presents evidence against our aspirations.

Such puerilities are in bad taste.

At the French House, discussing style over dinner makes me aware of the prevailing metaphor of *taste*. Mapping the sense of taste, composed of mouth-feel, olfactory response and memory, over the act of reading limits our conception of what belongs in fiction. The inclination to remove authorial presence – authorial body – from the work reflects minimalist trends in cuisine. A too-muchness in prose is parsed as greed or incontinence, which is unforgivable as bourgeois status displays are performances of disciplined appetite.

Will Self's style makes some readers queasy. It is too rich, his obscure vocabulary is chewy. That so many critical terms for writing resemble the review of a bad Sunday lunch highlights the cultural consensus. Why, I wonder, do we expect to devour a book? The logic of these metaphors leads to historical novels being stacked next to chocolate bars at the till. My mother would read her way through a pile of library books while picking at a bowl of grapes. As a child, I imitated her, reading heaps of science fiction novels while eating a Mars bar very slowly, making it last for chapters.

Will's confidence in his own style is shaken by the arrival in London of the American writer Tobias Wolff, also published by Bloomsbury, and his memoir *In Pharaoh's Army*, which covers his tour of duty in Vietnam.

'Tobias Wolff's style cannot be parodied,' explains Will. 'What if *that* is the mark of a good style?'

Wolff is an intimidating figure. For starters, he went to war.

I am invested in Will Self's style too. But whatever reassurance I offer on matters of style, I know that it will be ignored.

'Is this it?' he asks us. 'I am stuck with this style and these ideas, and I will repeat them on and on. Is that what happens to writers?'

The main course arrives, four works dropped in sequence: ptarmigan, skate wing, a pork chop, ox cheek. We eat and drink. Will continues to draw. Then our plates are cleared away, creating a broader canvas for him to work on. The drawings spread across the tablecloth, our words too, fragments of our conversation, the table talk written into the table. When the bill arrives, he offers the tablecloth as payment, half-heartedly, as if merely observing the trope of the impoverished artist offering artwork in lieu of payment, and with no expectation of it being fulfilled.

Leaving the French House, we move around Soho as if under a spotlight. He is unignorable on Frith Street. 'The thing with notoriety,' Will explains, 'is that everyone you meet remembers meeting you, and expects you to remember it too, and is offended when you do not.'

Meanwhile, two hundred miles to the north, in Blackpool, Tony Blair is delivering his speech to the Labour conference, his first speech as a party leader. Blair speaks for sixty-two minutes. His theme is change, inaugurating a new politics to come. New ideas and new thinking, a break with an exhausted Conservative government and a break from Labour's past. 'Ours is a project of national renewal,' he says, and closes with the fragmentary buzzwords that would characterise his style: 'Our party – new Labour; our mission – new Britain. New Labour, new Britain.'

The speech also signals his intention to break from Labour's commitment to public ownership of the means of production enshrined in Clause 4 of its constitution. In place of policy, there will be a statement of values, intended to guide the party through a changing society.

Night-time in Soho, we stride out from the French House in the direction of the Groucho Club, which Will tells us shall henceforth be called the Sealink Club. Offering no further explanation for this epithet, he stoops to light his cigarette, roaming the pavement like a question mark. Then he straightens up and becomes an exclamation point again.

El takes my arm. It is good to be young at a time like this. Young and new. She shows me the sign outside a fast-food joint, teaches me how to pronounce a word that is new to me.

'Not Phalla-phell,' she says. 'Falafel.'

She is planning to move to London, she says. The brother of a friend has offered to lend her the money for a deposit. There is a job going at the Thomas Cook in Berkeley Street. The pavement, greasy with rain, shines with neon light. I am where I want to be. We kiss. Can we do this together, help one another get on? Or will my ambition demand a betrayal?

There is a special party going on in the back room of the Sealink Club. We have tickets. Ambition is made spatial in the various nooks, floors, and private rooms of the Sealink Club. At our table, Beryl Bainbridge greets Will with affection. El talks about Liverpool with Beryl, who confesses that on her recent walk around Mount Pleasant she became quite out of breath. We are all intensely aware of our cigarettes.

'It's so hard to quit,' she says.

'I will quit,' says Will, leaning across the table, laying his hand on hers. 'If it helps you stop smoking, then I will stop smoking, and we can do it together.'

She demurs. He is serious. Adamant in fact. It is the right thing to do. He has quit smoking before, eating jar after jar of olives whenever he got the craving. The suggestion of a life without cigarettes seems impossible to me. For Will to suggest giving it all up seems like blasphemy.

The ashtray on the table is already full of our deathwork; of ashes and charred bones, silver foil and a single sticky black feather. Toward the end of the evening, Beryl risks another cigarette, and smokes it hesitantly, as if the cigarette might break apart at any moment.

ROUNDABOUTS

The driving school car pulls up in the rutted lay-by outside the cottage, Mike gets out of the driving seat, walks around, gets in at the passenger side. Mike waits for me. On driving lesson days, I'm scrupulously sober and therefore somewhat nervy. Mike is my servant but also my instructor. He is in his late fifties. The interior of the car is strikingly clean with an air of becalmed hygiene, like a waiting room. I haven't been in such a well-vacuumed space for some time.

Today is payday, a hundred quid in a white envelope left on Will's desk. I can afford a double lesson. From Will Self and his fictional topography, I've acquired a symbolic understanding of driving: from Ballard, I understand that car crashes are erotic, and that the modernity of the car constructs new desires; that is, technology such as the car reconfigures the human in its own image. From Will Self's story 'Scale', I am also aware of the motorway as a potential archaeological site for our descendants to explore and perhaps even use in their own religious rites. The car is freighted with meaning. It is a phallic symbol. It is a bullet. It is a screen onto the world.

As I mirror-signal-manoeuvre my way on the narrow lane, I tell Mike about my trip to London, and then ask him: 'Have you ever driven in London?'

He keeps his eye on the road, replying, 'No. We go to London by train. Me and the wife like to take in a show.'

The figure of speech amuses me.

'The phrase "to take in a show" comes from the late nineteenth century,' I say, 'back when people didn't go to musicals of their own free will and had to be *taken in.*'

Mike blanks me. '*Les Mis* was superb,' says Mike. Superb is one of Mike's words. His new conservatory is superb too.

I would like to drive in London. If I could drive in London then maybe when Will leaves the cottage and returns to the city, I can continue in his employ as chauffeur. I wonder if Mike is demonstrating a lack of ambition, by not driving in London. If driving was your thing, wouldn't you want to test yourself in the tough arena of London driving?

Today I am to be tested in the tough arena of the roundabout. The approach to Ipswich consists of a succession of roundabouts. I know plenty about the symbolic meaning of the roundabout. The word itself is far older than the circular junction it denotes. These traffic circles were originally termed *gyratories*; a letter to the *Times* in 1926 complains about this Latin term and advocates the stouter English word of roundabout in its place. 'Gyres' remind me of the WB Yeats poem 'Second Coming': 'Turning and turning in the widening gyre/ The falcon cannot hear the falconer.'

'It's very simple,' says Mike. 'Think of the roundabout as a clock and if you are leaving an exit that is past twelve o'clock, then you approach in the right-hand lane, with your right-hand signal blinking.'

This is where confusion sets in. The car, in passing clockwise around the roundabout, must first veer to the left – yet I am to signal to the right? In place of the usual logical sequence of driving, I am expected to make this conceptual leap that left, in this instance, means right; if seen from above, with a falcon's eye view of the situation, then I could understand the sense of it. But trapped behind the windscreen, slowing in anticipation of the junction, I am indecisive. At the entrance of the roundabout, I come to a stop.

Seeing a gap in the oncoming cars, I do not go; rather I make a mental note: that was a sufficient gap for me to drive through. Another gap comes and goes, providing further evidence of what constitutes a suitable gap in which to enter the roundabout.

'You have to be decisive,' says Mike. 'Anticipate!'

'By the time I've made my mind up to act, everyone else has moved on,' I reply.

I grit myself, close my eyes, and put my foot down. He makes it to his own brake just in time. We are now half-in and half-out of the roundabout. A dangerous place to be. Better to be all in and going with the flow. So I set off, going with the flow, but I'm in the wrong lane to come off the roundabout and so embark upon a second revolution. There are many meanings of the word 'roundabout' – it is an archaic expression for someone who doesn't get to the point, it is a type of dance, and it is an amusement ride. All three of these meanings could be applied to my traversing of the roundabout.

'Traffic is very complex,' I complain as we depart from one roundabout and head into another.

Mike is not amused.

'No, it's very simple. At a roundabout, you can go when there are no cars approaching from the right.'

'How can I be sure the other drivers are concentrating? How can I be certain they won't kill me?'

'You don't need to think about the whole roundabout. Concentrate on the right. Take your time, stay in control. You are in the driving seat.'

The driving seat is a clichéd metaphor for leadership, and a poor one at that; the driver is not a leader, the driver is passive behind the windscreen, making their small adjustments to fit in to the consensus of traffic.

Mike asks me about my family and I briefly sketch in the details before Mike gets around to the fact that Mike's father is very ill, and he is worried about him

'He's got a bad one. The lungs,' he says. I'm not so gauche as to ask him, *a bad what?* I know that older people don't like to say the word 'cancer'. They talk about the bad one or the one you don't get better from or, if you are lucky, the one that goes away, the one that responds to treatment. My gran died of cancer in our home, after being cared for by my mother Sylvia for months. I stood next to her dead body as her eldest son said a prayer, and throughout the whole sad time the word was never once uttered to me. Cancer, a fourteenth-century word derived from the Latin word for the crab, related to the Greek *karkinos*, the crab, and the Sanskrit, *karkata*. The word 'cancer' is a metaphor in which the slow death by uncontrolled cell division is likened to the creeping sideways movement of the crab.

You should never have a character develop cancer two-thirds into the story. You can tell a story about cancer if it starts with the diagnosis. But for cancer to constitute the fate of a character is dramatically unsatisfying because cancer has nothing to do with agency. We never deserve it. The irruption of cancer into our lives is exactly the kind of sudden violent metamorphosis that Will Self's characters undergo.

Will Self's pair of conjoined novellas *Cock and Bull* concerns two metamorphoses; in the first story, 'Cock', a woman grows a penis, in the second story, a rugby player grows a vagina behind his knee. As with Kafka's famous *Metamorphosis*, the fantastic is grounded within the mundane.

Will has a love for what he calls 'exploded metaphor', a phrase I first encounter in his review of Woody Allen's comic writing. 'The North London Book of the Dead' opens with an exploded metaphor for cancer: 'cancer tore through her body as if it were late for a meeting with other successful diseases.' That the word 'cancer' itself is metaphoric reminds me that thought and language are composed of junk metaphor, old ways of thinking hidden within the etymology of the word.

Mike is silent and mournful, thinking of his dad. His poor dying Dad. I slip into another roundabout, enjoying the sideways pull of the centrifugal force. Mike is so distracted that he lets me take another turn around the roundabout before I continue onward.

Metaphors change one thing into another, and by doing so, reveal previously hidden or unnoticed aspects of the thing being described. I've undergone a metamorphosis myself from Matthew Humphreys to Matthew De Abaitua. And what does De Abaitua reveal about Humphreys that was previously hidden or unnoticed? A strain of pretension, a yearning to be other than myself? Now is not the time for self-reflection. Mike is suffering. The moment calls for a homily. It calls for a metaphor.

'We're all branches on the tree of life,' I offer to Mike, by way of consolation. Wondering if it is the kind of thing that people like Mike say to one another to make themselves feel better. I can no more navigate Mike's cultural and emotional gyratory than the roundabouts of Ipswich.

Mike nods silently, doesn't expect me to talk more about his father, doesn't want to talk more about his father. I keep my eyes on the road.

'Life is a journey,' I say. Mike grimaces. Maybe, to a driving instructor, there are more inspirational metaphors than the journey. But I can't stop myself. Not now that I'm in the driving seat.

Learning to drive runs counter to the counter-culture of 1 Hall Cottages. Mike and his car sets me on the straight and narrow course. He will teach me about cause and effect. That driving, like life, is just one bloody thing after another. Whereas ideas come at me all at once and become merged and associated. They become metaphors.

Thomas Sprat, in his *The History of the Royal Society of London For the Improving of Natural Knowledge*, said that he wished to rid all scientific writing of 'this vicious abundance of phrase', by which he meant all figurative language, but metaphor primarily. Metaphor is associative, it connects previously unrelated objects and concepts, puts them in a relationship to increase our understanding of them. Metaphor is alchemical in the way it transforms base substances into aesthetic gold. It is magical thinking, mystical and irrational.

I am struck by one metaphor in particular, discovered in Will's copy of *Surrealist Games*: 'the sea is the night asleep during the day'.

The sea exists in space, and the night is a co-ordinate in time, but this metaphor creates an inky fabric of space-time. The sea and the night have a lot in common. They are states we enter into but do not inhabit. We know their surfaces but not their depths. Strange things lurk in them, fish and dreams.

The philosopher Julian Jaynes wrote that we understand something by finding a metaphor for it. The metaphor connects what we are familiar with to what has to be understood. He devised terms to explain this: the thing to be understood, he called a metaphrand, and the familiar thing, a metaphier. When we compare the sea to the night, both are familiar and understood, so it is not an interesting metaphor until we add the exploded component of the metaphor, of 'the night asleep during the day'.

The more I repeat this image, 'the sea is the night asleep during the day', the more the sea as a thing to be understood is replaced by this image of the night. Waves become the twitch and turn of a sleeper. The surrealist or exploded metaphor is more obtrusive than a standard literary metaphor. It overwhelms the thing to be understood, the metaphrand, with the otherness or unfamiliarity of its metaphier.

Will Self's short stories and novels are exploded metaphors – the afterlife is a suburb, waiters are writers, humans are apes. Metaphrands overwrite metaphiers, the lesser-known transforms the consensual and understood into something other.

Conventional metaphors make raw experience familiar. Exploded metaphors estrange us.

The scientific authorities counselled against metaphor. The metaphor is correlation – one things looks like another – and not causal. It belongs to a pre-scientific view of how the world works, to sympathetic magic and the philosophy of humours. But I am in thrall to it. Metaphor is so intimate, in the way it crosses over the senses, the way that it gives weight to ideas (that is, metaphorical heft is attributed to insubstantial concepts). Metaphors are baked so deep into language and thought that I exist entirely within their network of affinities.

Through the windscreen of the car, the expanse of Suffolk sky over flat plains is mystical. The clouds are metaphoric in so many ways I can barely keep my eyes on the road. Yes, I see shapes in the clouds due to the mind's habit of making faces out of random stimuli. Even the word *cloud* is a metaphor, derived from the Sanskrit *clud* meaning clump of earth, as if clouds are dirt on an otherwise clean surface. Clouds are contiguous with minds; in comic books, the thoughts of characters are encompassed by cloud-shaped bubbles, and to be lost in thought is to have your head in the clouds. I want to tell Mike about my revelation. I can't. The thoughts evaporate as soon as I conceive of them.

Because I have expended more effort in understanding the car as metaphor than car as mechanism, I am going to fail my driving test. Mike has tried to teach me about cause and effect but I can't or won't listen to him.

Turning and turning in the widening roundabout/ The driver cannot hear the driving instructor.

It starts to rain, and I turn the lights on and off before I find the windscreen wipers.

'The lesson is over,' says Mike. 'See if you can find the way back home without me guiding you.'

A SENSE OF PROPORTION

Milan Kundera writes that the novel is a form of consensual memory that protects us against the forgetting of being. He suggests that we need to be protected against forgetting, and this is true, where it concerns the underlying, unyielding facts of being. But it is also true that forgetting is merciful in sparing us the mistakes of our becoming. Forgetting quietens humiliation, it softens error.

* * *

Since his return from Australia, Will has been nursing an idea. Today he decides to share that idea with me. Inspired by the songlines, the great oral poems recited by the Aboriginal people as they walk the land, his plan is that he will, on stage, act out and recite his fifteen-thousand-word short story 'Scale' entirely from memory.

'Act?' I ask.

'I can act,' he says. He tells me about a play he was in. It sounds like the kind of plays children put on in attics. Also, given the impairment of memory caused by the special cigarettes, I am sceptical of his ability to recall the entire story. But he has a back-up plan and it involves me. I will sit on stage silently reading a copy of 'Scale' while he stalks the boards. If he forgets a line or word, then he can peer over my shoulder to remind himself.

'It'll be as if you're reading the story and I am your imagination,' he says with a thespian flourish. 'I want you to read out the parts of the text that are not in the first person – the chapter headings, the footnotes, the epigram. We will wear black.'

We begin rehearsing immediately. I sit in one of the two armchairs purchased from Mrs Franklin, our landlady. Going up to her estate to collect them made me nervous, given the unpleasant incident with her pheasant.

Each performance of 'Scale' will begin with the playing of a recording of John Major's speech to the Conservative Party Conference, in which the Prime Minister complained about the lack of services on the motorway.

'Every parent knows what I mean – "next services 54 miles" when your children can't make ten. They've got to go and those rules have to go.'

There is a pleasing mismatch in scale in Major's rhetoric; prime ministerial gravitas deployed to lament the measly volume of the infant bladder. Its proposal to do away with constraints upon the number of services mirrors the preoccupation of 'Scale' with the English motorway system. The unnamed narrator of 'Scale' is a composer of motorway verse and he has opiated fugues concerning the interpretation of motorways and their signage by far-flung descendants. Will Self's fictive method is to show how previously unrelated categories are contiguous: memory and motorway, writer and driver, the obsession of addiction and the compulsive behaviour impelled by the road system of the British Isles.

'Some people lose their sense of proportion; I've lost my sense of scale,' begins the short story. The story is divided into five sections, each of which explores a different meaning of the polysemous word 'scale'. In 'Kettle', the narrator injects himself with kaolin and morphine, and the chalky residue from the kaolin is deposited in his veins 'much in the manner of earth being piled up to form either an embankment or a cutting around a roadway.' In 'Relative', the narrator buys descalers for his kettle, reveals he has taken up residency in Beaconsfield model village, reflects on his career as a writer of crime novels set on motorways, and pretends to be a doctoral student writing a thesis on 'The Apprehension of Scale in *Gulliver's Travels*, with special reference to Lilliput.' 'The Ascent' recounts his motorway poetry, a recapitulation of oral literature 'analogous to the act whereby the poets of primitive cultures give life, actually breathe reality into the land'. The fourth section 'To The Bathroom' reveals that the narrator's marriage foundered on an act of adultery performed on bathroom scales. The fifth section 'Lizard' is narrated from a point in the future, in which the narrator has been physically and psychologically redefined in various ways according to scale.

The narrator's voice is highly performative, being an intermingling of academic pedantry with junkie demotic, opiated reverie and absurdist humour. Reading certain sections of the story, Will's face undergoes a subtle change; his chin retreats an inch, becomes weaker, in a satire of the pompous academic, and his words are heralded with empty moments of mastication and delivered with undertones of ineffectiveness. The narrator's various references to his father are deliberate barbs. The narrator's father is a critic of his work. '"There is no sense of scale in your books," he said to me shortly before he died.' In performance Will Self would also place a heavy emphasis on the '*died*' as he took pleasure in the narrative act of killing the father in this way, night after night (at this point, his father, Peter Self, was still alive). The narrator's father has a vision of fiction that cleaves to the nineteenth-century conception of the novel: 'Really important writing provides some sense of the relation between individual psychology and social change, of the scale of things in general.' 'Scale' is a baroque retort to this accusation. It answers the critique of a lack of scale with an angry superfluity of scale: bathroom scales, descalers, the scales upon a basking lizard. When the narrator insists that 'I must try and be more accurate with my figures of speech. I must use them as steel rulers to delimit thought,' I am reminded of Will Self's observation that his father Peter Self was 'a man who uses dialectics the way the Japanese used bamboo slivers during the war'.

The story is an argument between two ways of thinking, in Freudian terms, the polymorphously perverse against the controlling superego. As the story develops, the narrator perversely metamorphoses into the father. In old age, he may smoke morphine but it is from a pipe, that signifier of academic contemplation. By the time of the epilogue 'Lizard', set in the Lizard peninsula in Cornwall, where Will Self went walking with his father, the narrator is old and eminent, spending most of his time naked out on the sun porch like 'some moribund reptile'. Physically, he has acquired scales, and mentally also; in the place of the fugues and reverie of his youth, his attention is focused on microscopic events in an absurd rendition of academic specialism. The narrator apprehends the three separate levels of scale deposits within the kettle, and what they reveal about the nature of perception. From this position of repose, the narrator reflects on his youthful imagination, commenting directly upon the highly connective form of the story, in which various previously unrelated categories are brought into relation.

'When I was younger I could not focus on anything, or even apprehend a single thought, without feeling driven to incorporate it into some architectonic, some Great Design. I was also plagued by lusts, both fleshly and demonic, which sent me into such dizzying spirals of self-negation that I was compelled to narcosis.'

In other words: the father had a point. Without control, without steel rulers to delimit thought, the scale of ambition expands out of proportion to what the form can accommodate; the Great Design, the sense that everything is connected, is a grand generalisation, in which things are related by resemblance rather than by causality. It is the basis of metaphor, of magical thinking, of the intricate anti-systems of madness. The father advises caution in terms of ambition, and the story defies this counsel, disproves it through the thrilling voice and conceit, and then, by the end, admits some of the father's diminished proportions into itself. The lusts that plagued the narrator in his youth have to be subdued if he is to write. Middle age, with its reduced ambition, suggests a scale upon which the novel can be confidently erected.

As his amanuensis, I am aware of the story's oblique references to Will Self's own biography. The divorce and leaving of the family home: 'Guilt about my children... Ever since my loss of sense of scale, I have found it difficult to relate to my children.' Will's children visit the cottage now and again. We walk along the coast of Aldeburgh with them, and when they grow tired, he and I take a child each upon our shoulders. I am scared of the emotions entailed in the having and leaving of children, and at bedtime, I make myself silent and scarce. The children in Scale go unnamed, as does the ex-wife. The story inhabits the West London hinterland of the family, up and down the A40, with the narrator taking up residence in the model village of Beaconsfield, both in an attempt to appeal to the children and to revert to a childish state himself.

Will walks around the study, reading 'Scale' aloud, day after day. After rehearsals, I set the fire and we sit opposite one another in our armchairs. In the absence of television, I suggest we tell each other old storylines from *Eastenders*. Will takes this idea up, speculating that long after the fall of civilisation, the elders will sit around the campfire, a TV aerial as a staff, perhaps remote controls worn as necklaces, and relate the great oral history of the 'people who lived at the ends of the east'. In the early evening, with the fire glowing and books on our laps, he tries out other riffs on me; his comedy German, who may or may not be called Klaus, a persona built out of a single phrase. This is how Klaus works: I might make an assertion (it is always dangerous to make assertions in the cottage) such as 'I really like Vaughan Williams' evocations of the English pastoral' and Will huffs, clearing the way for Klaus to say, '*I think in Germany we do the English pastoral a little bit better than you do.*' No activity is too trivial for Klaus to patronisingly claim German superiority. Another example of Klaus might include:

Me: My duvet is covered in sperm.

Klaus: I think in Germany we cover our duvets in sperm *a little bit better than you do.*

In New York, Will Self takes a meeting with 'Saturday Night

Live' about Klaus, but nothing comes of it, and the character fades. But via Klaus and the rehearsals for Scale, it becomes clear to me that Will fancies himself an actor.

Bloomsbury, his publishers, book a series of 'Scale' gigs throughout November, opening at the National Theatre then off to Glasgow and three nights at Jackson's Lane next to Hampstead Heath; suddenly, the realisation dawns that our little cottage performance, and his fancy of himself as an actor, will be tested before a paying audience. The mood darkens. I anticipate uplift from the delivery of the finished copies of his new book, *Grey Area*, from the publisher. How will we celebrate? Perhaps with an after-pub drive across the fields?

The box of books arrives. Will rips it open and removes a copy. Although the publisher has forewarned him that *Grey Area* has not been bound as a conventional hardback but is instead, in a fit of design inspiration, ring-bound like an instruction manual, with a colour photograph of a tedious office interior on a cardboard cover, his disappointment is palpable.

(While we wait for Will's disappointment to build to fury, it's worth noting that no matter how modish or creative a concept the design department comes up with for a book format, every author wants the gravitas of conventional hardback publication. The author may smile encouragingly when the publisher explains how the flexible cover and small format will attract a new audience to their book, but they are crying inside. Anyway, back to the fury.)

Will shows me a copy of the ring-bound *Grey Area*.

'What do you think?' he asks.

'The form fits the content,' I say. Meaning that the title story evokes the boredom of office life, and a ring-bound manual is metonymic of office life (there are no ring-bound manuals in offices anymore, or need for instructions in any form, as office life is so contiguous with unoffice life that you may as well issue manuals for going to the pub).

'But don't you think it looks flimsy?' he asks again. All the good humour of the intervening weeks is gone. He opens the book then starts reading out 'Scale', exerting increasing pressure upon the cover until the spiral wires twist and the cardboard comes away in his hands.

'Flimsy,' he seethes.

I want to say, wait, don't. But it's not my role.

'Maybe it was just a defective copy. I will try another one.' Again, he flicks through the pages until he finds Scale, and starts reading. No sooner is he through the first paragraph than the collection of short stories is violently distributed across the room. He starts pulling out the books in armfuls, and now he is testing copies to destruction in quick succession, so that the cardboard covers lie torn between us and wire spirals are unbound.

'Open the other box,' he commands me.

I will not. I will not tear up Will Self's book. The destruction of books, and his books in particular, is one of the few issues in which I cannot remain ambivalent.

'Are you telling me I'm wrong?' he asks, accusingly.

Some people lose their sense of proportion.

Will Self warms up for the Scale performances with a reading in Brighton. On arrival at the gig, we discover that the organiser does not have any stimulants for Will. My small role in the performance is suspended. I am given an address and the keys to somebody's house, then take a taxi to their flat, let myself in, follow the directions to their stash, (a small envelope in an ethnic cabinet – because the police never think to check the ethnic cabinet) and then return immediately with the necessary.

I arrive back just as Tibor Fischer is on stage reading from his latest work, an uncompromising performance in which he reads the text and expects people to listen. Then Will Self is on stage, open-collared white shirt, black jacket, pallid and feeling the effects of whatever was in the envelope, his sibilants awry with the effort of righting himself under the yawing, pitching sea of drink and narcotics. I heard once that to imitate inebriation, actors overly enunciate their words, for nothing marks out a drunk like someone insisting they are not drunk. The gig goes well but I am concerned nonetheless.

The walk uphill to Brighton station is always demanding when you've been on the sauce and are chasing the last train. Pressed for time, we do not fit in the requisite amount of intoxication. While I sit in the carriage with Tibor Fischer, boring him rigid with the outline of a novel I may or may not write, Will waves a special cigarette at us and then lurches out of the train at Haywards Heath. He does not get back on. Gone, just like that. I wonder if I should get off at Gatwick and go back to look for him, but there are no more trains. Besides, my role is not to protect him.

The train pulls into Victoria station. Tibor and I disembark. As we are walking down the platform, I see Will standing nonchalantly outside the driver's cabin at the end of the train.

'Did they arrest you?' I ask.

'No. The driver caught me on the platform. He said, "You can't smoke that *there*. You can only smoke it in *here*," and he showed me into the driver's cabin. So I rode up front.' Will shows me the special cigarette, takes another drag on it. 'The driver asked if I wanted to drive the train into the station while he had a puff. And I did. *I drove your train.* It was exciting.'

'I can't believe he let you do that.'

'Well, huh, in Germany, *I think you'll find we drive our trains a little bit better than you do.'*

That night, I sleep at El's place in Acton. She lives with her best friend and two men in a shared house just off the A40. On a pair of mattresses on the unkempt floor of her dark bedroom, she tells me all about her troubles at work. She has a job as a cashier at Thomas Cook in Berkeley Square. El is up early next morning. I pull her to me but she is already dressed for work. Her red and blue polyester uniform gives off a subtle, static resistance.

She leaves me with a shopping list for dinner that evening; we will, as a couple, cook for the rest of the house. Acton is diffuse and centreless. For the first time in my life, I don't know what – beyond dinner – I am going to do next. On taking my position as Will Self's amanuensis, I accepted that the appointment would not last much longer than six months. It is mid-November. I started work in late July. I realise it would be wise to see what other opportunities are out there for a young man of my abilities.

I pick up a copy of the *Guardian*: at the time, the first and last resort for the arts graduate in want of employment. The job adverts contain the new buzz words. Employers are looking for candidates with a can-do philosophy capable of synergy and excellence, who can provide goal focus and growth assignments.

From a phone box beside the A40 I call the number on the media sales advert.

'I'm calling about the job.'

The call is transferred and a man, wearily rustling up a sheet of rote questions, begins the interview.

'What's your current position?'

'Amanuensis.'

'Aman-u-what?'

'Amanuensis. It's Latin for slave-at-hand. I'm a writer's

assistant.'

'OK. Do you have any experience of media sales?'

'I speak to journalists all the time.'

'Do you read the trade press?'

'The *what*?'

'The trade press.'

'Sorry, I'm next to the A40. It's very noisy here. What with all the cars. I didn't catch that.'

'Do you read *Marketing Week*? *Campaign*? *Media Week*?'

'What kind of man do you take me for?'

'It would help you in this position.'

'Why would I read the trade press for an industry I don't work in yet?'

'Do you have any experience?'

'I've published an article in a magazine called the *Idler*.'

'The *Idler*?'

'Yes, it's an anti-work magazine.'

Pause.

'Where would you like to be in five years' time?'

'On the dole but with more money.'

'That doesn't show much ambition.'

'I think it shows a great deal of ambition. It's incredibly difficult to sit around doing nothing all day yet earn lots of money. I'm a writer, you see. In five years' time, I'll have published my novel. I just need a job for the next few months, and I don't want to go back to being a security guard on Liverpool docks. Wait, I'm running out of money. Can I give you the number here, and then you call me back?'

I give him the number, and loiter beside the telephone box for an hour. I can't read people. I can't interpret their silences. The traffic on the A40 is incessant.

* * *

At dinner, I tell tales from 1 Hall Cottages. The other guests seem to enjoy my anecdote about the ducks on the keyboard, although the guests are not fully grasping the import of what I am trying to say.

'What are you trying to say, Matthew?' asks El.

I insist, 'That we are too ready to do what other people ask of us.'

El says, 'Does this mean you're trying to get out of the washing-up?'

'If we let ourselves be distracted then how can we hope to achieve anything?'

'What constitutes a distraction?'

'A job,' I offer. 'Domesticity. Everything in my life should feed into my writing.'

'What would you do for money?'

'Writing pays well. We mustn't let ourselves be carried away by the impetus of other people.'

El's good humour is gone. 'I don't know what you are getting at.'

'Changing my name was a way of making sure who I am feeds into my writing. Living in the cottage without TV, just reading books all the time, feeds into my writing. Anything that contributes to seeing the world in a more intense way helps.'

'What doesn't help?'

'*People*. Will referenced something Ballard said in the interview I transcribed: "when I was a young man, I would drive many miles for small talk." Social commitments can get in the way of writing.'

'What about relationships? What about us?' asks El.

'I've always felt that the stability of our relationship has allowed me to work without being distracted by jealousy and insecurity.'

She is furious with me. 'You make monogamy sound like Einstein wearing the same suit every day.'

I finish rolling the special cigarette and notice in the momentary hesitation of the other housemates that I am in breach of some sort of dinner party etiquette. I put the special cigarette behind my ear for later. In need of the toilet, I excuse myself and head out into the garden. There are no nettles in El's garden for me to urinate over so I find a suitable bare patch just beyond the patio. The fences between this row of gardens are low, indecently so. It is the lowness of the fence, its very unsuitability for urinating against, that makes me realise mid-piss that I am, again, contravening some obscure point of dinner party etiquette. The faces of the other guests, gazing at me aghast through the patio window, only confirm this suspicion. *People*.

El's bedroom is a converted living room with thick curtains over bay windows. There are two mattresses sprawled on the carpet, and clothes on chairs and a thin rail. She lies there silent with fury. I settle down next to her.

A publicist confides that the publishers are paying for me to travel with 'Scale' because Will is better behaved when I'm around, that he has a sense of responsibility toward me that makes him biddable. Our opening night is at the Cottesloe theatre, on the set of *Alice's Adventures Under Ground*, an uncannily convenient coincidence.

Will Self enters the stage bent double through a half-size door. I sit on stage, mostly silent and motionless, entirely content to play a figment of his imagination. After the NFT, it is up to Glasgow for a performance at the Tron Theatre followed by dinner with the novelist and artist Alasdair Grey – who we have been reading and corresponding with – at the Ubiquitous Chip. I am seated well-away from the grown-ups.

We return to London for the three performances at Jackson's Lane theatre in Hampstead Heath, and after the last one, Will descends into a gnashing fury. He drives the Citroën at full pelt through the twists and turns of a rat run. I'm in the passenger seat, with plenty of impassive expressions to hand, and a studied ambivalence toward the pressing question of survival. The two people in the back seat have far more to lose than I do: one is a young woman from the Bloomsbury PR department, and the other is a man who seems to be an old friend of Will's. His presence and every pronouncement only turns the screw tighter and tighter upon Will's unbiddable anger.

The Citroën vaults out of a side street, and we take a cuff on the wing mirror from a bollard for our impudence. The woman from Bloomsbury PR shrieks.

'Steady on,' says the old friend.

Will answers with 2.2 litres of fury. How fast is it possible to drive around inner London without crashing, I wonder? I look over at Will. I will not tell him to stop. I will not even suggest it. 'You have to understand,' he will tell me later, 'that you've had a happy childhood. And bad things haven't happened to you yet. But for me, when something difficult happens to me in the here and now, it sets off a chain reaction with all the trouble and pain I've had in the past, magnifying the difficulty, making it hard to control my reaction.'

At the traffic lights, he slams the breaks so hard that the unsecured passengers in the back tumble and roll against one another. The old friend quickly opens the back door, gets out at the lights and takes the woman from Bloomsbury PR with him. I get the feeling that whatever mollifying influence I may once have had is exhausted and that, as far as his publishers are concerned, my usefulness is at an end.

* * *

The next morning, I dial Will's number. He is staying somewhere in Shepherd's Bush. He sounds tired.

'Are you asleep?' I ask.

'Yes,' he replies, 'and you are part of my rather vivid dream, Matthew.'

OYSTER

The waiter lays a tiered platter of oysters and ice onto the red-and-white checked tablecloth. We have come to The Butley Oysterage for another one of my courses of instruction, our occasional sessions of Pygmalion. Will flicks his serviette so that it unfurls, every inch Max Weber's description of the Jewish man as an aristocratic pariah with a patrician streak. I take up a half-shell, sever the foot which connects the quivering bivalve to its carapace, then tip it into me along with a glug of seawater. Salty, raw, watery, the pleasure of oysters is entirely metaphorical.

Will pours the wine and considers what that metaphor might be. Is it cunnilingual? Yes, oysters are an aphrodisiac and these are calcified labia that we are levering wide open. But there is more to the metaphor than the merely sexual. Oysters were long seen as a poor man's luxury, protein to bulk out the meat in Lancashire hotpot. But, in the early Nineties, oysters are upwardly mobile, a Tony Blair of the bivalves. Working class tradition served on a silver platter. And what is the reward for such triangulated ambition? To be eaten alive!

Will slurps down another oyster, uninhibited, entirely committed to the act.

'*La petite mort*,' I say.

To eat oysters is to exult in our power. Our power over bivalves. The epilogue of *My Idea of Fun* is set in the Oyster Bar beneath Grand Central station in New York, the same bar in which Will Self interviewed Bret Easton Ellis: you can follow the logic of that choice of location, for both Easton Ellis' novel *American Psycho* and *My Idea of Fun* conflate serial killing with consumerism. Ian Wharton's florid murders are a way of internalising contemporary power, in much the same way that primitive man consumed the brains of chieftains to keep their knowledge within the tribe. In the epilogue, Ian Wharton takes his infant son to the oyster bar and the child slurps down two dozen oysters, 'wielding his fork like a connoisseur.' The child is the Fat Controller reincarnated, the embodiment of appetite's voracity, he is capital made flesh. (In nineteenth-century slang, oyster meant profit or advantage.)

'I'm always in a state of desiring oysters,' says Will. Oysters and desire. Martin Amis, in an interview with Will Self that I transcribed, relates an anecdote concerning Norman Mailer. The punchline is delivered by the object of Mailer's impotent *amour*: 'it was like trying to fit an oyster into a parking meter.' This vivid simile appears in Martin Amis' *The Information*, a novel published in such a nimbus of gossipy, high literary imbroglio that I had to promise to make only one copy of the transcript and hand it over in a plain brown envelope to Will in person in the Sealink Club.

The oyster is desire, then, and if the world is your oyster then it is a world entirely responsive to your desires. The happy solitude of the oyster, a world unto itself, until that world is so rudely shucked by reality.

If I can discern the meaning of oysters perhaps the true purpose of our dinner in the Butley Oysterage will become clear to me.

Whenever Will teaches me something, it is very much in the sink-or-swim school of pedagogy; he is half-annoyed that he is paying for the privilege of delivering my education, and half-sad: his children should be the beneficiaries of his teaching. Yet he is in exile from them, self-imposed or otherwise. Exile interspersed with frequent trips to the heart of the city.

We work our way up the tiers of oysters. The higher levels of adulthood are hidden from me, I never see what is coming, not with any accuracy. A free-floating, nebulous anxiety stands in for realistic predictions concerning my immediate future. There is always somebody more adult than you, insofar as adulthood is derived from experience rather than knowledge, from *having done to others* and *having had done to you*. Will schools me in social mores (not least that they are pronounced *more-rays*) but I will have to wait a long time before I can access the hidden upper tiers of adulthood, the deals to be made with money, the price of guilt, the shortening odds of death. It's frustrating, as a young man too proud to admit to ignorance, to know that on some matters – that is, on the important stuff – you cannot be taken seriously, regardless of how wide or arcane your reading.

With the oysters put out of their misery, our napkins scrunched up and deposited along with the discarded shells, the waiter's suggestion of a second bottle of wine rebuffed, and a resolution for coffee made, Will gets down to business.

'Do you remember that when we first spoke about the job, I

said it would be for six months.'

I do the sum and give him the answer, 'January.'

'After Christmas, I won't be able to afford to pay you the hundred quid a week. I need to cut back on the New Glib and start writing fiction again. I'll pay you fifty quid a week.'

I nod. Of course. It's entirely fair. No problem. I will cut my cloth accordingly. It does not occur to me that he is asking me to leave the cottage.

The New Glib is Will's term for the meretricious, self-reflexive comment demanded by a booming media to fill its burgeoning pagination. The term is scrawled on one of the Post-it notes in the study. The thing is, the New Glib really *pays*. There is dash and dare in how little one can get away with for so much money. In my time at 1 Hall Cottages, Will dedicates time and effort to his journalism, seeking the validation of professionalism while resenting the media, emotionally and intellectually, for its failings, its complicity: if I make an assertion as to the relative ethical merits of one newspaper over another, he corrects me by intoning that 'a newspaper is nothing more than an advertising medium predicated on its circulation'. Book reviewing fulfils the obligation to contribute and therefore sustain a literary culture; the integrity of long-form journalism is buttressed by research and interviews, but the New Glib, with its loosely strung-together anecdotes, generalisations from personal experience and riffs, is indicative of the decadence of the period, a decadence that has gotten into his blood.

He has not written a word of fiction since I arrived. The novel called 'Good' has been abandoned. The cover was to feature a middle-class mother with a shopping bag in one hand and a semi-automatic weapon in the other, and the story concerned intra-borough warfare on the streets of London. But fiction has been deferred, over and again, for the New Glib.

The financial inducements of the New Glib are especially tempting because Will has so many *fucking people* dependant on him; he adds up his dependents for my benefit, including not only his estranged wife and children but also his wife's new partner, their cleaner, his agent and accountant, our cleaner Glynnis, Col the gamekeeper and our occasional gardener and, of course, me; together, we are a pyramid of stunt skiers balanced upon his shoulders, forcing him out again and again to perform.

The next day, during breakfast, the *Evening Standard* calls to request an article on Christmas shopping, and this seems to Will to be the ideal pretext to coin more New Glib. By the time I have cleared the table, brewed and served coffee in the study, washed the dishes, urinated and smoked in the garden, Will has written an article entitled 'All I want for Christmas is a bonfire and a bag of magic mushrooms.' His article calls for the restoration of the pagan nature of the winter festival; the article is too out there for the *Evening Standard*, and Will knows it. The rest of the morning is expended in negotiating the kill fee.

This hurried, botched piece is indicative of a new mood in the cottage, a turning away from the twin performances of New Glib and promotional readings. The writing of fiction requires private focus. I will be an ongoing distraction to the obsessive attentiveness required of the novel.

There are other distractions, of course. Will rechristened the Groucho Club the Sealink Club for its resemblance to a roll-on, roll-off ferry. The metaphor is unpacked in the novella *The Sweet Smell of Psychosis*: 'It is the raised sills of the doorway, together with the functionalist decor of the establishment – naked bulbs behind wire basketry, bright orange floor coverings, steel furniture bolted to those floors – and the persistent humming judder which perfused the place, that had gifted it its name… But more importantly, to be in the Sealink *was* to be at sea – in more senses than one.'

The Sealink Club is a private joke that becomes a minor landmark in Will Self's fictional topography, and it is synonymous with the New Glib. *The Sweet Smell of Psychosis*, published in 1996, concerns a provincial young man's induction into the high media cult of the New Glib. In *Great Apes*, published a year later, the artist Simon Dykes and his lover Sarah take cocaine in the car deck floor of the Sealink while upstairs their friend Tony Figes assails a journalist with theories about the New Glib. The scene is a repugnant fugue of drugs and drink, adults behaving like unsupervised children, naughty on narcotics and botched sex. Orifices are clogged, watery cocaine mucus mingles with vaginal musk. Self-disgust and vituperative satire intermingle. Gussets are soiled. The Sealink and Simon's addictions are contiguous, one flows into another, and that perhaps is what it means to be all at sea, the uncertainty that comes from being carried away by the tide of the times.

Will is the Sealink Club's most ardent critic, he visits it over and over again to confirm his worst suspicions; he discovers the Churchill, a martini so strong it quivers on the verge of becoming a gas. Caught in the torque of his contrary impulses, exile and return, repelled by the acts of decadence he is compelled to perform, he is the mad pirate captain of the Sealink, determined to run it onto the rocks.

In *Great Apes*, Simon Dykes lolls at the bar of the Sealink Club, a convivial bivalve sustained by the nutrients carried on the currents of conversation. Will Self retools this image for the introduction to his second collection of journalism, *Feeding Frenzy*: 'The world is my brine – I am an oyster: a literary bivalve, cemented to the sea bed, extracting whatever nutriment I can from the ebb and flow of the popular unconscious.' The rise of gastronomy in the Nineties is symptomatic of the era's decadence, with food displacing the arts as an arbitrary index of bourgeois attainment, a high culture of low urges. The Sealink Club, oysters and the New Glib form a triumvirate of empty greedy mouths, the maddening fin de siècle round of talking and consuming.

A cold wind direct from Siberia rattles the windows of the cottage. From the master bedroom comes a fusillade of coughs followed by Will's strangled cry of 'I just don't feel like it today!' Will has returned from the Sealink, and after the gab of the bar comes the brooding silence of the cottage. I take Montaigne down from the library, find the lines from 'On Glory' that I had read the night before: 'we are, I know not how, double in ourselves, which is the cause that what we believe we do not believe, and cannot disengage ourselves from what we condemn.'

I set the fire in the study but Will does not appear, and I sense that my presence is the reason. I should ask him about it. But I cannot. Emotional candour is not in my repertoire. The furious silence from upstairs makes me feel like a child again, when my father would work nights, and we were instructed – on pain of severe sanction – not to wake him. We could not make a sound, and so I would entertain myself with the muted unfolding of nine hundred pages of Ceefax. Lacking a television in 1 Hall Cottages, I distract myself with the transcripts of the tapes Nelson sent to me, overheard conversations are the only conversations left for me. I begin cutting up and rearranging their words, looking for clues as to what I should do next. One phrase reoccurs. I write it out twice: 'Don't stop'.

Home for Christmas. Eddie and Sylvia want to know what I plan to do next with my new name, and for how long I will remain at 1 Hall Cottages. I have a plan of action. I will borrow a Super 8mm camera. I will recreate moments from our dreams and film them. This is how I will make myself indispensable in the cottage, this is how I will deny the shame of being a stalled son.

In the pubs and clubs of Liverpool, I bump into old school friends. Drunk and shouting over the sound of revelry, I spell my new name out for them: De-a-BAY-thua. Nobody has heard of Will Self. Nobody is exercised by issues pressing upon the contemporary novel. Why am I still doing school work in my early twenties when I should be out there earning like a real man? You can't be a student your whole life. You have to live in the real world. You've made the mistake of dedicating yourself to doing something you love. In the real world, we find things we hate and we do them badly for the rest of our lives.

But I want to be a writer.

But what if it doesn't happen for you? What if you try and fail?

(And my life will be made up of success and failure. Mostly, I will be a nearly-writer. I will waste years in over-ambitious and over-complicated narratives. Insufficient moral and emotional ballast as a young man means that I create unappealing characters. I will pay too much attention to what I can earn, banjaxing Plan A with Plan B. I will fail to pay attention to people. Failure is the common experience of writing. We hear from the few who succeed, but just this once let's hear from the nearly-men and almost-women of the world, their hearts dusted with the grey sediment of steadily eroded dreams.)

The insufficiencies of my hometown are a spur to ambition. Maghull is a suburb best appreciated at thirty miles an hour. At walking pace, its attenuated streets merge with daydreams of glory and escape. At twenty-two years old, I'm still young enough to feel a keen nostalgia toward home, the intensity of returning to the place I grew up in but no longer belong. This intensity will fade over time, the act of coming home will become familiar, and one day, even if I recognise, buried in the grizzled jowly countenances of the men at the bar, the boys I once ran with, we will have nothing to say to one another.

The town's Lancastrian heritage can be enjoyed by walking south along Poverty Lane, over Summerhill, between the playing field of my old primary school and a pig farm opposite. The fences around the school are much higher than they used to be. Cut across Balls Wood, head past Morton's dairies, (my brother-in-law still delivers door-to-door for them) then up Bootle Hill to the Bootle Arms, where, in my late teens, I worked as cellar boy, mucking out the Dobermans and lugging up the crates and kegs. Attain Melling Mount and look out across the greenbelt and motorway to where the misty tower blocks of Kirby give the finger to the Lancastrian bucolic.

How many times must I take this walk across my lifetime? How many times will I trespass upon my boyhood?

OWEN & I

It's hard to write truthful stories when you are young because you don't know how things will turn out. How it ends. You cannot discern the pattern of the future in the grain of the present. You are stuck in-between. Beginnings are all you know, and so either you make the rest of it up, or you stop writing.

* * *

I am nine years old, up at half seven, before my parents or siblings. I sleep in my vest, Y-fronts and socks to save time. On the chair, where I folded them the previous evening, are long trousers, a white shirt and a narrow green-black-and-white tie. On the cusp of the Eighties, rationing still echoes through British life, especially in Liverpool. My mother cuts my hair with her father's thinning scissors. Sunday night is bath night.

I meet Owen on the corner of Croftfield at a quarter past eight. We set off on our walk to school. Fog drifts over Glenn Park, obscuring the length of Eastway and its recurring two-storey semi-detached houses. We walk through a silent memory of front lawns, bare rose bushes and pebble-dashing, the addictive scent of creosote lingering in the fresh damp air.

The lollipop lady escorts us across Poverty Lane. The streets are quiet apart from the busy silken whirring of the milk float's battery-powered engine. Frost skeins persist in the shadow of the kerb. Our senses are so innocent that we can be overwhelmed by peculiar intensities. I know which grids, when levered up, pour forth ants from the underworld. When I am fed leftovers, I can smell who ate first from that particular plate.

Owen is the fastest boy in the school yet he is nagged by doubt, and preoccupied with finding his faults in others.

'I've seen you cry,' says Owen.

'No you haven't. I never cry.'

'That time on the field you cried.'

'You sat on my chest and rubbed grass cuttings in my face.'

'You cried.'

'I didn't.'

'You did.'

(Let us resolve this argument, once and for all, nearly forty years later. I did not cry when Owen rubbed grass cuttings in my eyes, nor did I cry when he chewed up my best pencil, or picked my rubber apart.)

I never cried in front of anyone. Owen did. Owen's crying got worse as he got older and I would often see him red-eyed in class. He was sensitive to criticism, a terrible affliction for a boy growing up in Liverpool in the Seventies and early Eighties, when the city was a national pariah, and its sole export was cruel banter.

Summerhill is a modest bump undercut by the local railway line. We cross a footbridge lined with corrugated iron panels covered in graffiti; a panel has been wrenched aside so that, if we dare, we could slip through and go down onto the embankment and then the railway line itself with its lethal third rail.

The train rumbles underneath the bridge. Owen and I grip the top of the corrugated iron sections and dangle there, our feet scrabbling free of the vibrating walkway. We look at one another, checking that we can both endure the test. The train passes and we let go and land back on our feet. My fingers are scored by the thin edge of the corrugated iron panel.

On the other side of the bridge, the path runs alongside the school playing field. Straight hundred-metre running lanes are painted upon the long grass, next to the white markings of a football pitch. The wooden goalposts, broken during a big boy dare, have been replaced by metal goalposts which knock unwary players unconscious. When the heavy waterlogged leather case of the ball strikes the metal posts, they toll.

Vandalism and graffiti are the works of the big boys, their anarchist sigils and words obscure to us; what is a Pink Floyd, how does one Zappa? Repairs after such vandalism are designed to punish everyone, like a halved portion of communal gruel. Classroom windows, punctured by a ball bearing fired from a catapult, are covered over with chipboard for an entire term.

Beyond the western corner of the playing field, there is marshland, owned but unloved by the railway company. It is our edgeland, where we build dens, fight with sticks, and tie rope swings over murky pools of fetid swamp water, obeying an obscure impulse for a rite of passage.

Owen sees some big boys crossing the bridge.

'Dare you to call them names,' he says. Owen is made out of dimples and mischief.

I walk faster. I plead with him not to dare me. I hate dares and their unnecessary risks. He dares me. But I won't do it.

Boys are afraid of their own cowardice but love to discover it in others.

Owen turns round, faces the big boys and calls them the rudest word he knows.

It's on. The chase. Or, as it termed in High Scouse, the *legger*.

Owen is the fastest runner in the school, and in a couple of years, he will be – briefly – one of the fastest runners in the county. In my dreams, I still run like a boy, untiring, up and down empty lanes, fast. But never as fast as Owen. Sports Day is a race to finish second behind Owen.

Owen is already five yards ahead of me and we've only just started. I call out for him to wait but he keeps running.

What happens next happens so suddenly that I can barely recall it. Hands grab me, lift me. I am in the air. An out-of-body experience. The big boys heft me up and throw me over the fence. I land on the other side in the grass among broken bricks. The indignity knocks the wind out of me. I'm bigger than my friends; in my more fanciful moments, I believe I can – one-handed and at arm's length, like Darth Vader – pick up the smallest boy in the infant class by his throat. I have all the moves planned out if I am ever set upon by a gang of ninjas. But I don't have time to put a single one of my moves into play before I am chucked aside like a bag of spuds.

I get up, climb miserably over the fence and trudge down the quiet lane. The big boys run back the way that they came. Owen waits for me. He is my best friend and he makes my life a misery.

Owen tells the teachers about the assault. I'm not really bothered and would prefer not to make a fuss. I am accustomed to being hit. My older brother Andrew is sixteen and attacks me every day to 'toughen me up for my own good': when I beat him at Subbuteo he shouts 'crowd violence' and attacks me with my mother's perm comb. He sits on my shoulders and drools over my face. To avenge myself, I wait in the wardrobe and, when he quietly cracks open the door to secrete his cigarettes in the pocket of an old blazer, I rise out of the dark and grab his wrist. He almost faints with shock. Compared to this daily diet of sibling brutality, being chucked over a fence is neither here nor there. But as far as the authorities are concerned, a line has been crossed.

The next day, a posse waits on the railway bridge, led by the school headmaster. Owen and I are there, as are my mother, Sylvia, and my father Eddie, the plain clothes detective, who is making a rare appearance in the land of children. Eddie wears a sheepskin coat, the wool lining sour with the smell of stake-outs and the cigarette smoke of the Toxteth dive frequented by his snitch. He doesn't belong here. He doesn't really belong anywhere. He will be preoccupied with *the job* for my entire childhood.

(In class, I imitate Eddie's habit of staring off into space; I don't know that he is thinking about the job he has just come from, the murders, the bodies, the awful things. All I know is that he is staring. So I stare meaningfully at the middle distance until Owen asks me why I am being so weird.)

With this posse, we wait. The big boys approach. Owen recognises them. To be honest, I don't. But there aren't many big boys who walk this way, as Poverty Lane leads in the opposite direction to the secondary schools.

'Is that them?' asks the headmaster.

'Yes,' says Owen.

'Are you sure?' my mother asks me.

I nod.

The big boys gain the bridge. The headmaster steps out in front of them.

'Now, boys, I want to speak to you about something that…'

And this is all that the headmaster gets to say before he is interrupted by the quick darting movement of a sheepskin coat. 'If you ever lay a hand on my son again…' is all I hear. My mother shields me from the unpleasantness. She assures the headmaster that Eddie will not actually throw the boys off the bridge. The recollection of the headmaster's panicky face at the sight of Eddie chastising the boys, in the manner of Regan from *The Sweeney*, always made my mother laugh. The whole incident is something I often forget, and when I sat down to write today, I wasn't going to start at this point. Now I realise this scene was crucial. But not for me. For Owen. It is only through the story of other people that I can tell the story of myself.

We're on the swings at Glenn Park. Two of the four swings are broken. The seesaw has been stolen. The roundabout also. The slide is wet with long streaks of rain and Big Boys' piss.

Owen has a holster and a pistol from the TV show *The Professionals*. We play war. We practise the irrecoverable magic of knowing when an imaginary bullet hits or misses. We spend all day in our imagination, building dens that stand in for prisoner of war camps, or taking turns to die in spectacular fashion under a remorseless assault of Zulus.

There are other boys around here somewhere, and every few weeks Owen, out of tyrannical insecurity, will initiate a shift in the alliances between the pack: the ruddy cheeks of tall Simon Hooten (Si), with scar tissue down his calves from a babyhood accident with boiling water; slight Steven Horrocks (Ozzie), with his great big back garden; Jeremy Tisdall (Tizzie), the best footballer of the bunch (Nicknames use that same suffix of -ie, so Jeremy Tisdall becomes Tizzie and Michael Sarath becomes Sazzie. Nicknames are our grubby mythologies: no-one knows where they come from and they never go away); Jamie (Jamie-*ie*?), whose Dad is on the rigs (the family spent time in Venezuela and returned with the American affectation of openly declaring their love toward one another. Our cruel imitations of 'Love you Dad, Love you Mom' soon put paid to that.) Little Spencer, who never stood a chance with that name. Dave and his cousin Kevin, our enemies, a class thing. Owen has a scar on his thumb where Dave once bit him to the bone. During the same fight, and much against my will, caught up in the momentum of the dare, I hit Kevin so hard his nose would not stop bleeding. I had to pacify him by giving him all the *Flash Gordon* cards stashed in the lining of my parka. Ten years later, Kevin will try to exact revenge by chasing me across a night club car park over the roofs of parked cars.

On rainy days we play war in Owen's dark house. On the mantelpiece, there is a posed black-and-white photograph of Owen at four or five years old, dressed as a cowboy, with a white bandana covering the lower half of his face and a toy rifle in his hands. This photograph is very important to his sense of self: it's not make believe, it's evidence of the kind of man he could become.

Upstairs, we bang around from bedroom to bedroom or, if left unsupervised, the living room becomes the barracks of a prisoner of war camp, with blankets strewn about. Female nurses, in the form of teddy bears, visit us. Owen has his favourite teddy bear to cuddle up to and kiss. I must make do with Nookie Bear.

Nookie Bear is a celebrity at the time, appearing frequently on light entertainment shows as the cheeky puppet of ventriloquist Roger De Courcey. Nookie wears a rosette on his bearish breast and his general demeanour is that of a local councillor who is four Scotches into celebrating re-election. If you pull a string in the back of Nookie's head, he goes cross-eyed or *gozzie*, the first silly face a boy learns to make.

I kiss Nookie, press my body against him, cradle his head in my hand and gently, teasingly, pull the string so that he goes gozzie with ecstasy.

Yet, on my part, the encounter is unsatisfying.

The rain clears. We itch to be out of the house. We go around the estate, knocking on doors. A whole pack of us roams the estate behind Glenn Park, looking for bored big boys to goad. Owen is always the one who starts it. He gets in close, right in their faces, and then the *legger* is on. We scatter like starlings, down alleyways and through cross-hatched wire fences, skidding away atop the wet tarmacked garage roofs.

Owen has perfected a high yodelling call, and when he feels the chase is lagging, he will yodel to bring us out of our hiding places so that we can prowl after our pursuers and goad them into making a greater effort. Seeing me thrown over a fence by the big boys has only increased his appetite for the legger, for his need to prove himself.

* * *

We know the big boys from what they leave behind: cigarette butts in the grass next to the swings; the broken wire fence around the bowling green, pressed down low for a kickabout on the immaculate turf; rubber johnnies in the hedge; the glimmer and stench of broken vodka bottles on the concrete slopes under the flyover; the piss streaking the metal curve of the slide.

'Do you realise that I could beat you up and all your friends at the same time?' says my big brother Andrew. 'Ten, fifteen of you. You wouldn't be able to touch me.' He has a dark wedge fringe and keeps a knuckle duster in the secret compartment of the cupboard. He sleeps on one side of the room, I sleep on the other.

'Luke Skywalker is a homo,' he mutters, just before falling asleep.

Andrew incites me with a number of nicknames: Blake (because I was once seven years old and liked a TV show called *Blake's Seven*) and Wehttam, which is my first name spelled backwards. I play football with him and his friends. They live on Monster Munch and pints of milk and drive out to Wales to break into Butlins. Andrew kicks the ball hard. I dive and block it.

Andrew says that Owen cries so much because he hasn't been toughened up. He hasn't had the end of a rolled-up magazine jabbed into his face or a Kays catalogue brought down across his back. You have to be careful what you say to Owen, and this will be true for as long as I know him; he will push and goad and annoy because he has no experience of retribution. Owen's older brother is a gentle soul.

* * *

Dinner time in the school hall, with tins of cabbage, fish fingers and mashed potato delivered to each table by the dinner ladies. We are the servers, doling out a portion to the six other young children on the table. If one of the younger children refuses their food, Owen and I squabble over who gets it.

'Where were you born?' asks Owen. 'Ormskirk or Liverpool?'

If I tell the truth and say Ormskirk then I will be a *woolly back* for the rest of my life.

'Southampton,' I say. 'My parents were coming back from a

cruise.' The lie seems to impress him. Perhaps I should do more to cultivate an air of exoticism?

* * *

We call it 'the swamp' – a few acres of marshland between Summerhill playing field and the railway line. It is a place for dares, like the opaque, slow-witted water of the Leeds-Liverpool canal that runs through the town.

Big boys have slung a knotted blue rope over a high branch. Owen dares me to swing out over the marsh and back again, half-heartedly, because he knows that he would not have the courage to follow me if I did. To be a coward was, in the terms of High Scouse, to be a *whacker*, an epithet accompanied by a quick mime of flatulence.

We set traps in the marsh, small spiked pits and trip wires which, when snapped, release taut bent willow branches. In the empty heart of a rhododendron bush, we crouch and plan. Could we live here? Owen can get some sausages if I can get some matches. We weave young green branches together to make the walls of our own little world.

Sometimes we see figures in the marsh. Grown-ups. We know them from their leftovers too, torn pages of pornography and empty whiskey bottles. *Tramps.*

We play out from morning to night. Manhunt, football, war, den-building. By sundown, my legs ache, I am sick with hunger and thirst and home seems so far away. The narrow secret paths through the marsh are dark, and the way back is uncertain. Heavy, lazy motes of imagination drift in the low sun. I come through the high reeds and find myself on the opposite side of the deep swamp water with the blue rope swing. A thin shirtless man with straggling dirty hair is on the other side, rummaging around under a charred fallen log. Owen is nowhere to be seen. Hiding, probably. The man climbs up a tree. I walk around the swamp and when I find the courage to look again at the tree, I see only stout crows on the branches. The man has gone, broken down into his constituent avian parts. A birdman.

I clamber over the broken fence and run across the playing field. Owen's shadow runs ahead of me. I call out for him to wait but he keeps running.

* * *

Liverpool Football Club is the best team in the world. Managed by Bob Paisley, they win the European Cup or the League or both every year. Never the FA Cup and that always rankles with me. The team is consistent in its line up. Ray Clemence in goal, Phil Neal, Alan Kennedy, Alan Hansen, Phil Thompson, Steve Heighway, Sammy Lee or Jimmy Case, Terry McDermott, Graeme Souness, Kenny Dalglish, David Johnson.

I'm fascinated with the players who never or rarely make the team: Kevin Sheedy, who would later excel for Everton; the forward Howard Gayle – Liverpool's first black player – who rattles Bayern Munich; the mysterious Frank McGarvey who arrives for a princely sum and never plays. As a goalkeeper myself, the player I'm most intrigued by is the rarely-glimpsed reserve keeper Steve Ogrizovic. The exoticism of the surname notwithstanding (it's Serbian), it seems to me that whenever the ball shoots past Ray Clemence and into the back of the net, then Ogrizovic would have stopped it. Ogrizovic is the shadow self, the hidden potential.

Legends like Kenny Dalglish don't interest me. I want other realms. I want Ogrizovic on the pitch. I want a line-up of occulted players. Colin Irwin. Richard Money. Frank

McGarvey. The shadow squad. What is the origin of such gnostic inklings? A younger brother wandering away from the straight and narrow path set by the father and the eldest son? Or is science fiction to blame – all those dystopias and apocalypses, speculation about the way things could be instead of the way things are? Too many comics? Probably. I will later interview three of my favourite writers from the science fiction comic *2000AD*: two were active in the occult and the third was on his way to join some kind of coven. Things are not as they appear to be, I know that much. I need a mentor who can instruct me in this other realm. A birdman. An Ogrizovic.

* * *

We go up to senior school in our big ill-fitting uniforms. Owen and I are allocated different forms and so our friendship is put on hiatus. The boys coming in from other larger primaries are rougher, and cooler. I grit my teeth and do what must be done: I sell my collection of *Star Wars* action figures.

Saturdays are spent prowling around newsagents for comics, then to the library where I am working my way through the science fiction section and Terrance Dicks' novelisations of *Doctor Who*. I hide my comics in the wardrobe in case another boy comes over and sees them. Comics are childish, a sign of weakness (absurd now to think that an eleven-year-old boy would be embarrassed to own a copy of *The Avengers* comic. Thirty years later, watching *The Avengers* film with my five-year-old son, the twenty-somethings around us shift uneasily: why has that man brought a child in here?).

Owen curries favour with a different crowd, the boys who find being themselves an effortless natural state. Not a bad crowd. They're not the really bad boys, the ones from known families – that would be Clive (Cock of the Year, 1980–1983) or the vicious Patrick (Cock of the Year 1984–85) who sits on a boy's head and makes it crack against the playground.

Sideburns are shaven ruthlessly upward to above the top of the ear, ties are worn thin and short. Shoes are slip-on moccasins, brogues are stamped-upon spoonies. I spend my playtime foraging in the grass verges for lost coins. I tell the other boys that I've become a binman and a new nickname is coined: Binman Maff. (I meant to say that I'd put the binbags out for my mother but was suddenly taken by the image of myself as a binman, riding on the side of the truck like a cowboy, and thought it would add an air of exoticism.)

I never say anything to my parents about my unhappiness. Andrew, in a rare moment of big brother protectiveness, senses it and resolves to sort it out.

He arranges a fight for me.

Andrew tells Jamie that I've been going around saying that I could beat him in a fight. Jamie is a big Sylvester Stallone fan. I feel sick and nervous beforehand because I hate to do the wrong thing. 'I will not fight him,' I say, when approached by Jamie's seconds, 'but if he chooses to attack me on my way home from school then I will be forced to defend myself.' Fighting is wrong, a waste of effort. No good can come of it. My survival plan for my school years consists of keeping my head down, getting a raft of qualifications and buggering off – and any effort contrary to this goal is superfluous.

'Fight! Fight! Fight!' chant the ring of children.

Jamie spent too much time in America. He is fat. His nipples wobble at the end of two soft cones of flesh. The entire fight consists of him trying to hit me and me dodging around asking him to stop. The children, bored by the absence of blood, wander off. Andrew, furious on the sidelines, orders me to finish it so that we can go home for dinner. I push a tired Jamie to the ground, lean over, and rap my knuckles briskly but tentatively across his face. It's enough. I'm done.

Jamie and I chat amiably enough on the walk home. Andrew promises to fix me up with a better opponent next time.

* * *

I'm fifteen. A miserable year. Raw and unformed, and gloomy about sex. Nuclear apocalypse would, perhaps, offer me some hope of getting laid. My sexual fantasies begin with the four-minute warning and end with three minutes to spare.

Scallies attack me all the time. It might be personal but I don't know what I've done. Nothing. That's it. I've done nothing. Apart from being fifteen.

As I'm walking home from my friend's house, a car slows and a man throws an empty pint glass at me. It sails by and smashes off a brick wall. Men spill out the Everest pub at closing time and immediately saunter over, offering me *out*, a suitably ambiguous phrase. A fight or a fuck? You learn the hotspots, over time. The places to avoid. The people to avoid. I can spot trouble from a hundred yards simply from the swagger of its silhouette. My walks home begin to take oblique routes. Psychogeography: mapping the hang-outs of the psychos.

Don't get me wrong. Some of my best friends are scallies. Like Joe Bury, whose Dad leaves out porn films for us if we babysit Little Bury. For one glorious summer I will corral Bury and the rest of his scally mates into a functioning *Dungeons and Dragons* group, and they spend days wandering my imaginary realms. Instead of shoplifting confectionery and duvet covers to flog down the market, Bury lifts a *Monster Manual* and a compendium of *Unearthed Arcana* for me. In the evenings Mr

Bury smokes cannabis with his brother while Mrs Bury flirts with us boys. It's an exhausting way to live, with the Burys; you're always on your toes because it might, at any moment, *kick off*. In the end my authority as Dungeon Master is compromised when Joe Bury's twelfth level cleric dies in a way I thought would be dramatically interesting, with resurrection planned further down the line. Joe takes it badly, goes to the kitchen, fetches his mother's vegetable knife and presses the blade against my throat.

'No-one kills me in my own house,' he hisses.

* * *

Throughout my childhood, a siren sounds at nine o'clock every Monday morning, a test in case an inmate escapes from Ashworth hospital on the outskirts of Maghull. Behind the high walls of this high-security psychiatric hospital, home to Moors Murderer Ian Brady and other violent mentally ill criminals, there are lavish sports facilities: an indoor football pitch upholstered with Astroturf, a gleaming gym with cricket nets and rowing machines, and a full-sized outdoor football pitch with floodlights/spotlights. Why do the inmates of Ashworth high security psychiatric hospital have a full-sized football pitch? What terrifying Sunday league do they belong to?

Our boys' team, Glenn Park, has no facilities. In hard times, our manager, Mick, has shown entrepreneurial talent in securing kit and sponsorship from the local garage. Now he goes one further. He gets the boys access to Ashworth's facilities. We will train there on Fridays and then, on alternate Sundays, use its full-sized outdoor football pitch as our home ground, overlooked by the cells and wards of mentally-ill and violent criminals.

Before a game, we meet outside the security gates. Once everyone is assembled, Mick calls over a guard and we are led inside.

Bags are forbidden. The guard, a burly Lancastrian in a dark navy-blue uniform and peaked cap, groups the boys into sixes and counts them into the double-gated, airlock entrance. Football boots in hand, we are quiet and tense. The demons from the news live here, rippers and stranglers named after their catchment areas of Cardiff or Essex.

I'm guessing the reasoning for having a teenage boys' football team play their home matches in a high-security psychiatric hospital holding the country's violent criminals went something like this:

Mick: Why should the psychopaths have all the good facilities and the children have nothing?

The Authorities: Ashworth has an image problem. Maybe if we let children play football in our high-security psychiatric hospital full of violent criminals, then public opinion will turn in our favour.

The opposition arrive in a motorcade of windowless transit and mini-vans. The back doors swing open; the boys, nauseous after a half-hour crammed together on benches inhaling diesel fumes, stand pale and shivering against the high walls. Dumb and compliant, they too are counted into the airlock; a rival batch of boys, gobby and gawky, not fully tuned into the signals of adulthood, so receiving garbled transmissions concerning sex, girls and personal hygiene. No parents attend the games; it's far too early on a Sunday morning for that. The spectators, that is, our home support, are a dozen or so people who stand dutifully in an allotted area on the touchline.

The game is played in an atmosphere of fearful restraint. The boys run gingerly, reluctant to put their full weight upon the earth, as if running around in somebody else's house. Yelps of exertion echo across the compound. The play is congested, the lads reluctant to run down the wings and get some chalk on their boots. On the touchline, the small crowd confer among themselves, like a panel of judges at a talent contest.

Talk about a psychological home advantage.

My boots are far too small for me and so I can't kick the ball. Our captain, Steve, who does not believe I should be in the team at all, jogs reluctantly back to hoof the ball up field. In goal, I feel lonely and exposed and I don't have a good game.

Later that week, training on the Ashworth Astroturf, after I save the second of his penalties, Steve walks calmly over and knees me hard in the groin. I go down in pain. Mick rubs my shoulders. It's the third time a member of my own team has violently fouled me in training. I never react. It's not worth it.

'Why are you rubbing his shoulders, Mick? He was kneed in the balls.'

Mick says, 'Well, I'm not rubbing those.'

After training, we are escorted quickly through the corridors. In the airlock, the boys discuss a party. They are laughing about somebody. About Owen. Fat Owen. The class clown has become their figure of fun. Owen showed up at a party wearing a waistcoat. It had been agreed that all the other lads would be wearing their waistcoats too, but they weren't, because they didn't own waistcoats, they had only pretended to, and so, in front of the whole party of teenage Scousers, Owen burst into tears and ran away with his maroon waistcoat undone. I remember the way he used to cry, the way his face reddened and the tears brimmed in his eyes, and he couldn't hold it back, no matter how much he tried to hide it. His big back shuddering, the tears coming quicker than he could wipe them away. He had been the fastest boy in the county but he has put on so much weight that his body clock stopped cold.

Owen is the last to pubescence. We've all run on ahead and he's yet to catch up.

I know that he has a kind of girlfriend, El, and has lied about the things he has done with her, selling out their friendship to impress the people who hate him.

And how do I feel about Owen's fall? His terrible spotty obese adolescence? Not much. I am fifteen years old and hardly capable of emotional nuance toward someone I was friends with four years earlier. A veritable eternity. It's been all change around here, and a much-desired change to the self is always accompanied by a change in the company it keeps: as Rilke writes in *The Notebooks of Malte Laurids Brigge* (first issued in English under the title of *The Journal of My Other Self*), 'What's the point of telling anyone that I'm changing? I haven't remained who I was, I'm different from who I was before; so, clearly, I have no friends or acquaintances.'

* * *

Coming up for a corner, another player – one of theirs, maybe one of ours – punches me in the solar plexus so hard that I end up in the back of the net. With the final whistle, I quit the team. I'm tired of spending my Sunday mornings in an institution, playing a joyless game with violent boring lads for the entertainment of a crowd of people I don't know.

Walking wearily home across Whinney Brook field, I spot Owen walking his dog. We talk. We get on. There is a kind of disbelief in his face.

'Why did we stop being friends?' he says.

'You wanted to hang out with Percy and Steve.'

He winces.

'Wankers,' he says.

The hiatus in our friendship is over.

* * *

Everything changes in Sixth Form. The wankers leave school, a whole tier of our society moves on to knock up girlfriends, get married, develop drug habits, and work in shops, building sites and local solicitors' offices. Adolescence settles down. I no longer walk the streets with my head down. Owen finally gets his double dose of testosterone. He takes up running again, loses all the weight, but not the dimples.

The uniform is different in sixth form, not quite so grey. On a school trip to Paris, a Swedish girl licks her lips at me. The field is clear for us to bring our desires to bear.

We talk about girls.

'Who do you fancy?' he asks.

Owen is popular with the girls. He has his eye on one in particular, Lisa. And before he asks Lisa out, what do I think of her best friend, his former girlfriend, El?

Just like that, the unthinkable happens. Owen sets me up on a double date with El. We become a foursome. In Sixth Form, everyone pairs off in a most grown-up and conventional fashion. These first relationships are strong bonds; many will end in marriage, then divorce.

The foursome go on nights out. At a quiet Quadrant Park, Clive In The White Wig, a dancer from the nightclub-based TV show *The Hitman and Her*, performs while we drink double Drambuie. I wear chinos, a smart shirt with a paisley tie, and a jacket with enormous shoulder pads – an outfit more suitable for a job interview than a night out.

I never have *a good night out*. This is not what I want. This is not who I want to be.

'Don't you wish,' observes Owen, 'that there was a pair of trousers we could wear other than chinos?'

'What about jeans?' I ask.

'You can't wear jeans to a club.'

'Black jeans?'

'You can't wear black. Students wear black. I *hate* students. What have they got to be so miserable about?'

Over the course of a weekend, these terrible nightclubs – Quadrant Park, Coconut Grove – are transformed into heaving, loved-up raves. We stop going. Youth culture has arrived but it's too late for us. We go to Fallows instead, in a light industrial park. Fallows is a cut above. The scallies call us the Kylies and Jasons, bland and uptight young fogeys.

For my eighteenth birthday, we wear our new suit jackets. Owen's jacket is a deep red with maroon sleeves, and he has chosen the buttons for his shirt especially: Alison May, who is not his girlfriend, has sewn them on for him. He is fastidious about his appearance. No, fastidious is the wrong word. That implies a dandy's confidence and self-assurance. Owen's confidence is a conspiracy we must all participate in; one splitter, one dissenter, and the whole edifice will come crashing down.

I am broad-shouldered and my bottle-green jacket makes me look like a head balanced on a snooker baize. My shirt, a gift from El, has some nice stitching on it. Owen wants to know the most times we've done it in a night, and whether we do this or that, and do El's hands move when I make love to her?

We drink Drambuie. The dry ice comes up. You're a fake, sings Alexander O'Neal.

* * *

I look for my true self in the stalls at Quiggans, among the counter-cultural flotsam and jetsam still washing up after the wreckage of the Sixties; the carved wooden Buddhas, incense sticks, hash pipes, Tarot cards, Hendrix t-shirts of the alternative state of mind. Tracksuit bottoms now come with paisley turn-ups. I buy a mustard-coloured hooded top with Aztec geometric patterns. I write poetry in the pages of a plastic Filofax and read the *NME*, searching for the music of my self. I watch *Rumblefish* and it makes me want to stop people in the street and ask, why have you let your self go?

My mother sews a Public Enemy patch on the back of a black hooded top, which I accessorise with a leather Africa pendant. On Sandhills station, surrounded by the desolate docklands and the cold wind blowing in from the Mersey, I brood, sumptuously alienated.

The closer we get to the final exams, the less I see of Owen. He stops coming to school and works more shifts at the greengrocers. We're drifting apart again. I'm studying hard and preparing for the undergraduate life to come but he's not going anywhere. He's staying. I'm leaving...

...And one day, I'll come back triumphant and stride down the streets of Maghull in my father's sheepskin coat, a pork-pie hat, an orange shirt and lime-green jogging bottoms to defy the chino-wearers who stayed behind. You may have a job but I have literature! You may have a sovereign ring but I have a puzzle ring! And I will drink at all your familiar haunts, and hang my coat up at Charlie Cs for the duration of a pint, for as long as I can stand to be among you all, and when I collect my sheepskin coat, ostentatiously bored of the brutish tedium of the same old faces doing the same old things, I'll discover that the coat has been slashed with a razor neatly and entirely down the back...

Instead of revising, Owen goes on long runs. He's training for the police physical. He comes over to speak to my father about *the job*, and though Eddie does not give *the job* a ringing endorsement – it's changing, he says, it won't be like the old days – Owen leaves convinced that this is what he wants. The uniform. The sense of belonging. The strength. The heroism. Picking up two lads by the scruff of their necks and banging them against a corrugated iron wall. He'll serve his time as a bobby first and then move over to the CID for the serious stuff.

Owen hangs out with his brothers' friends. After the exams are over, we go to the Alt together. The Alt pub is so rammed on a Friday night that it's difficult to move, never mind talk. Why come to a pub where you can't talk? I'm bored of standing around, arms pressed close, taking tiny sips from a pint glass (Owen forbids me from drinking bottled lagers because my big hands diminish the potency of the bottle and its label for the rest of the lads. I know, I know).

The crowd mills outside on a warm night. It's the last summer of school, the end of my childhood, and instead of a rite of passage, some Ferris Bueller yawp of defiance, I am sat there listening to the lads talk about fuckin' this and fuckin' that. Then I fucked her, the fucking fuck.

I interrupt the lads. I've been keeping my head down for eighteen years. I've been punched and mocked and never kicked back because I was playing the long game. The coward's game. Anyway, the lads look wearily at me, and, a little drunk, I say, finally: 'If you insist upon using fuck as a noun, adjective and verb in the same sentence then I find it difficult to know what the *fuck* you are talking about. If you stopped swearing, and considered the substance of what you're actually saying, you will realise that you might as well be quacking like a fucking duck for all the sense you make.'

* * *

I see Owen once more, four years later. Home for Christmas from 1 Hall Cottages and I bump into him at the Alt. I tell him the story about Will and my new name, and he seems happy for me. For ten minutes we talk amiably and put all past striving and competition behind us. He didn't get into the police, not right away. A heart murmur. His blood pressure was so high when he first took the test that they had to send him home. He stuck at it, though, and they let him in. Tells me he doesn't like working the beat on Friday nights when the scallies are out, and that surprises me. Because what are you doing in the job if you're not getting stuck into the scallies?

It was good to finally catch up.

Yes, it was. It was.

* * *

I think about him most days. Hanging by our hands from the corrugated sections of the railway bridge, two little boys, asking each other: how am I doing? How are we doing?

Not so well, Owen, to be honest.

The people you leave behind, the life you reject. Old friends are signposts down an untaken path. Ambition requires betrayal.

Owen died at the age of thirty-seven, after a long period of absence from the police force. I don't know how he died, and at the funeral the circumstances surrounding his death are unclear to an outsider like myself. There is a photograph of Owen on the front of the order of service. His face is unrecognisable and monstrous.

What happened to him?

In this photograph, Owen leans over the back of his son. It's like the man is trying to hide himself behind the boy. The coffin, when it is brought into the crematorium, is a broad hexagon.

Because it is a police funeral, my father Eddie, retired, sits next to me. After the service, he talks to the other police about Owen. He had been a diligent bobby. One detective remembers Owen taking an excellent witness report, best he ever saw, but, afterwards, Owen rang the detective in the middle of the night to check the report was OK.

Such a need to please, such uncertainty about the self – it's not going to help a policeman in a city like Liverpool.

The police he served with speak fondly of him at his funeral, of his practical jokes, his Benny Hill impression. But I know, by the end, that he hated the job. It wasn't what he'd wanted at all. I can't look at the photograph of him any longer. I turn the order of service over and there, on the other side, is that black and white photograph of Owen I remember from his mantelpiece, when he was four or five years old, dressed as a cowboy, the lower half his face covered with a bandana, holding a toy rifle.

* * *

Sports day. The grass is dry and sharp. On Summerhill playing field, the boys line up at the start of the running track, straight white lines daubed on long grass. We are far out, at the edge of the field, with the marshes at our backs and the distant hubbub of parents and other children ahead. I look along the line of boys. We sway on our marks, we freeze to get set, we go. I run. I run fast, then faster still. There goes Owen, running ahead. I can never. Never reach him. I call out for him to wait but he keeps running.

HOW THINGS END

Promptly after New Year, I leave Maghull and arrive back at 1 Hall Cottages to resume work. Will and Victoria are in the study; it is clear from their reluctant greetings that they did not expect me back so soon. January blues. No appointments in the calendar, no deadlines for me to hit. I sit parasitical in my bedroom. What else am I to do?

I return to the transcripts of the conversations Nelson recorded at his pub, and try to shape them into a story. Stories have a beginning, a middle and an end. Life is mostly middle. To be *in medias res* is to suffer a constant nervousness, driven by the anxiety engines and stoked by the fear furnaces. It requires a leap of faith or a cruel act of ambition to force an ending.

Even my driving instructor senses my subdued mood. As I fail another hill start, he asks me if I am feeling up to it. I ask about a test date. If only I could drive, I could make myself useful again. Soon, he promises. But it won't be soon enough. At my request, he drops me at the entrance to an alternative school in the area. My plan is to walk directly up to the school and offer my services as a writing tutor. But my courage fails me on the driveway. My plan is ridiculous. But what else am I to do, where am I to go? Back to Liverpool, back to where I started from? I am stuck in the middle.

Back in the cottage, El calls and we talk. She is still cross with me for my behaviour at the party in her house, my cold remarks about our relationship. But she hears the shadows behind my silences. Will and Victoria are off again for a few days. She is willing to put aside our argument because I am in urgent need of company. El will come over, bring friends, cheer me up. The next day, a little gang of twenty-somethings shows up at 1 Hall Cottages in a small car. We drive out to Sizewell, to Aldeburgh, to all the meaningful places. But, with the onset of winter, their meanings have gone cold. After a day out, we return to the cottage. El holds my hand and feels the vibrations of the anxiety engines, the heat of the fear furnaces.

There is a message on the answering machine. Will is returning to the cottage earlier than planned. He is returning today. But the cottage is full of my friends. I should turn them out, immediately, and sweep the grate and ready his house for his return. But I don't. I leave a message for him in turn.

'Just to *warn* you that I have people here,' I say.

He calls back.

'Just to *warn* me?'

'That I have people here.'

'You don't get to *warn* me, Matthew. It's my house. It's where I live. You don't *warn* me about coming back to my own home.'

I have fucked up.

El stands there as I pace around the study.

'It'll be OK,' she says.

'How? How will it be OK?'

'You had to have friends over. Being on your own all the time is making you sad.'

'It doesn't matter what I want. My needs are unnecessary.'

Will finds other accommodation for the night. The next morning, my guests leave. I am too busy clearing the ashes from the fire grate to notice. I kiss El goodbye as my friends get quietly back into their car. They can see that I'm in a bad way. Fifty a quid a week to live like this. They pity me.

'It'll be alright,' says El. 'It's never as bad as you think it is.'

Her hand at the back of my neck. Life can't just be about books. There must be people too. But how am I going to cope with people? I don't know anything about people. *People* are the problem.

Alone, I go out into the cold bare fields. The box with the raven's wing is empty, the copse where I killed the pheasant is a wicker cage of denuded branches. Col the gamekeeper is holed up in his terraced house somewhere, thawing out the last of his goose. Such fleeting connections, there is nothing to keep me in this place.

When Will arrives back with Victoria, I am holed up in my bedroom, wearing my headphones, working on the tapes that Nelson sent me. Rewinding and replaying certain sections of conversation over and again to ensure my transcription is accurate. I think I have enough to begin writing. I plan a story about three young men in a car on their way to a party. The driver is on drugs and they don't have a map. In the story, they drive around and around the city, getting more and more lost, sinking deeper into their own private lagoons of hallucination, to the point where not only do they forget where they are going, they also lose track of where they came from. Writing the story takes all night and into the morning. It's the only piece of fiction I complete during my time at 1 Hall Cottages. Now and again, a voice cuts through the dialogue spooling through the headphones. A voice from downstairs: it is Will shouting at me, and Victoria mollifying him. I hear him say, 'while he hides away up there in his room like an adolescent.' But I feel strangely calm. Just before turning in, I find a title for my story: 'Inbetween'.

The next morning, I wake up and realise that I have to leave 1 Hall Cottages. My time as amanuensis is over. I've been avoiding accepting it because I have no idea what else I will do with my life but that is not a good enough excuse to hang around once the job is done. I will do the honourable thing. I go downstairs.

Will is making coffee in the kitchen.

'I think I should go,' I say.

'Yes,' says Will.

'I rang my driving instructor and told him I'm leaving. That's it, really.'

He is relieved, I can see that. I'm sparing him the unpleasantness of turning me out onto the street. I guess that he never considered, when he decided to employ a live-in amanuensis, how on earth he would get rid of me when I was no longer required. And who really needs an amanuensis anyway: was the job merely part of his dream of what it would be like to be a writer, to have someone to handle the unpleasant tasks while he got on with the inspiration? Someone to unpack the bags he could not bear to touch? You can't delegate those kinds of tasks. That's one of the hidden levels of adulthood – the day you realise that you have to do all the important stuff in life yourself, and there's no ducking it.

'I will go now,' I say. 'I'll come back some other time for my stereo. I'll call a cab.'

'No,' he says. 'Let me drive you to the station.'

One last time in the Citroën. And the thing is, freed of the burden of being my employer, my landlord, proxy parent and occasional mentor, he can talk honestly on that drive, and we can laugh about it all, because it's over. You have to finish things. You have to learn how things end. Otherwise you get stuck halfway on the road to revelation.

'Are you going back to Liverpool?' he asks.

'No. To London.'

'Do you have someone you can stay with?'

'Yes. It's all sorted,' I lie.

At Saxmundham station, we say our goodbyes. By volunteering to leave, and by doing so immediately, I feel that I have rescued something between us. We shake hands, or perhaps we even hug it out, I can't remember. Then Will hands me a matchbox.

'This is your redundancy package,' he says.

Inside the matchbox, folded in a neat arrangement, there is a cheque for a hundred pounds, a pair of freshly-picked psilocybin mushrooms, and the makings of a final special cigarette: our time together rendered on a miniature scale.

I take the train to London because that's what you do when you have nowhere else to go. On the concourse of Liverpool Street Station, I meet the winter city with nothing more than a rucksack of clothes, a notebook, a typewriter and the matchbox containing my redundancy package. I descend into the Underground station. On the platform, indigestinal gases from deep in the body of the city circulate ahead of an approaching train. The passengers agitate toward the edge. I board with them. Londoners move obediently through the carriage and arrange themselves according to an etiquette of discreet distance. You belong to a city only when you know its rules of public behaviour. I hang off a strap and rock along with the rolling stock. As a newcomer to London, my observations and experiences are generic. The only aspect of London to which I can claim any particular knowledge is the borough of Will Self, or its perimeter at least: Bar Italia, a particular Chinese restaurant on the edge of Chinatown, the upstairs and downstairs of the Sealink Club, the quiet streets of East Finchley where he grew up.

From the vantage point of early middle age, after a lifetime working and living in London, every face in this city is familiar to me. The pressure of the city knuckles the faces around me, shaping diverse lives into singular expressions – I crave, I want, I am thwarted, I fail, I hate, I forgive. Even if I do not know these people, then I recognise their need. Even if I have not walked every street of the city, then I have walked a similar street. My London moments come with a vague sense of déjà vu, a time-echo of a half-forgotten night out or a bygone business plan. In the fleeting reflections in the high glass windows of office blocks, I glimpse the long-abandoned projects pitched to me by people I have forgotten. Oh, the innumerable schemes and escape plans of Londoners pressed upon me! They change with the times. It used to be novels and books of every stripe, or magazine dummies and internet sites, and then it became the endless apps and the ideas for game shows and erotic musicals. As a young man I loved ideas for the new new thing. Now I dread them. London demands scheme and hustle: the scams to get into school catchment areas, the career strategies, adultery tactics, and fucking kitchen refurbs. The fumes given off by ambition blowing hot and cold.

You have to keep moving. With my typewriter and my bag of clothes, I walk across Whitehall, running my hand along the blunt points of black iron railings. The bottom storeys of the offices of state are barely inhabited. Power does not lower itself to the level of the street.

I move on to Hyde Park. Nannies in scarves and gloves, a different ethnicity from the children they care for.

On the Mall, a man wearing the sleeves of his sweater knotted around his chest, in the southern European style, climbs in to a sports car and revs the engine, even as his long-legged girlfriend climbs into the passenger seat. Their aristocratic whippet, spooked by the sound of the engine, rears back from the car. The man in the sweater revs the engine again, and she leans out through the open door to gather the dog up in her arms and bring it into the car, but the dog is too gangly, and it trots backward and shakes its head as if to say, no, not with him, *not again*. And she promises the dog that it will be different this time, that he will be different this time. The dog submits to being hauled on board, and the sports car pulls noisily away, the passenger door still half-open.

I find myself on Piccadilly, typewriter under one arm, bag of clothes weighing down the other. The Ritz. Then an expensive car showroom. I go into the bank and cash my redundancy check. I have a hundred pounds to my name and will have to find work. Through the smoked glass window of the bank, I watch dispatch riders stream in the gutters between the lines of vehicles; self-styled anti-heroes, satchels slung over their backs, insinuating themselves into the narrow channels of traffic.

Dispatch riders are citizens of Will Self Country, featuring in the story 'Waiting' in *The Quantity Theory of Insanity*. The protagonist Jim is obsessed with traffic – 'Jim', I guess, as in

James Graham Ballard. He falls in with a dispatch rider cult led by Carlos, who wears the regulation jacket and bright vinyl tabard of his profession. Carlos takes Jim through traffic, demonstrating 'an unnatural facility' to anticipate the stop-and-go of rush hour's improvised system:

'Carlos had not only apprehended every road, he had anticipated every alleyway, every mews, every garage forecourt, and the position and synchronisation of every traffic light. He could not possibly know what he seemed to know – the only way he could have seen the route we took was from the air, and even then he would have had to have made constant trigonometric calculations to figure out the angles we seemed to have followed intuitively.'

Carlos' ability is a perfect prediction of sat nav, albeit in mystical form: echoes of future technology pulse back into the present, where they are interpreted as magic. 'Waiting' riffs on the heightened psychic state of the riders, their ability to detect nuance in the collective unconscious of traffic, and this speaks to a truth about their subculture: the dispatch riders are counter-cultural types with white boy dreads, Cornish wizard's beards, tribal piercings. Their body odour is herbal from summers spent in Goa, experimenting with DMT, dancing to trance music in fractal t-shirts. They move quickly through the stalled brain matter of the city, silvery synaptic transmissions of magical thinking.

The city cannot abide a low-velocity presence. Counter-culture or mainstream, it's all a matter of pace. The dispatch riders move information around; before broadband, data was encoded on zip disks or burned onto CDs and carried around the city in couriers' satchels. The harder the city thinks, the quicker they pedal. Outside a pub, a flock of bikes rests after a long day of connecting. I ask a rider if he has a contact number for the agency, someone I can call to get work. He writes the number in my notebook.

My other option for employment is to become a security guard. In the lobbies of the banks and financial services, behind revolving doors, and tucked well away from the beautiful women on reception, stationed perhaps behind the giant aluminium pots holding the rainforest flora of the atrium, there I will lurk in uniform, watching the necessary people come and go.

Late afternoon and I arrive at my destination: the Thomas Cook in Berkeley Square. I wait on the other side of the street from the entrance. Writing is a solitary activity. Will Self is clear on the matter: if you cannot stand your own company and are incapable of sitting quietly in a room for eight hours a day, then you cannot be a writer. When he was at 1 Hall Cottages, he maintained a workaholic writing schedule; all day at the desk, knocking off early evening for a couple of large Scotches to read back over the drafts. This image of the solitary writer persuaded me that if only I could divest myself of my responsibility to other people then I would discover the necessary discipline to write.

When I said this to El, at her dinner party, it opened up chasms of doubt in our relationship. You think you know somebody and then they come out with something like *that*.

My arms are tired from carrying my stuff. It is as dark as a London street gets. As the night deepens, the city grows unfamiliar. Part of me knows that I am not ready yet to be a fiction writer. The ambition is there, the persona is there, the name is there. But the work isn't. The only thing I know is that I belong with El. I thought she was part of my past, that our relationship was generic; the big city breaks up provincial lovers. But that's not the way it has to be. Or should be. I realised it on the night at the French House, when we kissed under Soho neon. Here, we can change together. Stories are about change, it is life's constant. But you can't write about change until you've experienced it, both in yourself and in the people you love, and the people you hate, and that's why it is so hard to write a decent novel when you are young. I thought that if only I sacrificed something I loved then that would be a rite of passage into becoming a writer.

Ten minutes before the office of Thomas Cook is due to close, a limousine pulls up delivering a prince and his cohort. They are my age, though their wealth makes them look older. I watch them go in. The preparations to close up for the evening are put on hold for the prince. Often the young princes show up like this, at the last possible moment, to collect half a million francs for a weekend in Monte Carlo, and so the cashiers have to stay late.

The prince and his entourage leave with their briefcase of sharp notes. When El eventually emerges from her shift, her hands are sore at counting out their money. My form is indistinct in the winter gloom. She sees me, stops, says goodbye to her colleagues and crosses the street. I don't know if she is annoyed to see me or pleased. I can't read her expression until the last moment.

'You're here?' says El.

'Yes.'

'What happened?'

'I decided to leave Suffolk. It's fine.'

'What are you going to do now?'

'I'm sorry about what I said. I didn't think.'

'You never think about my feelings.'

She's right. I have to be more considerate, not let ambition turn me into somebody I don't need to be. The street is dark, our faces are barely visible to one another, so when El speaks, it is as if she is talking from a shadow hidden within her. I listen. I hear her. All the time I've been trying to catch a glimpse of something meaningful out of the corner of my eye, I've denied the real world its due. Ambition, intoxication, dreams, books – I have used them as ways of ignoring the world.

'Can I stay with you?' I ask, shifting my typewriter from one arm to the other, tall, strong and helpless.

It is a cold evening in January. The shops are extinguished. People are leaving the city for home, their silhouettes streaming down this dark street toward the light of the main drag. A pigeon limps in the gutter. Just a pigeon, a simple desperate bird, nothing more than that.

'Of course you can stay with me,' says El. She stands on tiptoe and we kiss and hold one another. And though, from appearances, we may look generic, as two newly-minted Londoners, between us there will be stories entirely of our own invention.

SPRING '97

The *Idler* office is on Farringdon Road. Not an office as such, but a partition within an outpost of the *Guardian* diaspora. The editor, Tom, the art director, Gavin, and myself, the intern, work on a trio of wheezing Macs surrounded by boxes of unsold back issues. For months, other *Idler* interns have come and gone; for them, the unpaid glamour of the media palls quickly when a friend of the family offers them a job in the City. For me, this is all I ever wanted. To write, to be published and possibly even to be read.

I collect the odd scrap of evidence that the magazine is being read. A letter from the notorious MP Alan Clark demands biographies of the *Idler* writers: who is this Matthew De Abaitua, he asks? Does he have any credentials? Must I listen to his opinion? Does he have – in the words of Tom's mother, Liz Hodgkinson – 'bottom'? 'Bottom' is a fat ass of learning and gravitas, a solid base on which a commentator's opinions are founded. I don't have 'bottom', at least in the metaphorical sense. In my notebooks, phrases such as 'The Home Counties are the Source of All Evil,' and articles in praise of all-night garages are indicative of the meagre gravity of my ass.

The editor Tom agrees to pay me thirty quid cash a week and meets my demand for a pack of oatcakes and/or oat-based bar for lunch. My time at the *Idler* indoctrinates me into a way of office life that is – to the best of my knowledge – now extinct. There is no PowerPoint. No minutes kept at meetings. No appraisals.

The *Guardian* is keeping an eye on us, just in case we turn out to be Bright Young Things. A brief item in *Private Eye* questions whether we should be allowed near a national newspaper at all, describing the magazine as a 'one-joke Will Self fanzine staffed by friends of the former junkie.' They point out that Matthew De Abiteau (their spelling. Possibly some kind of joke?) is not even my real name, and they accuse me of really being someone called Matthew Collins. We are put in with other young people creating sections and sponsored bits and bobs for the main paper. Massive Attack, Radiohead, Manic Street Preachers are playing on the office stereo. There are ashtrays on the desks. I am invariably late for work but what do you expect when you employ The Idler?

I complete the short story I drafted on my final night at 1 Hall Cottages. It is titled 'Inbetween' because I still feel like we are not there yet. Being a twenty-something in big media's final hours is a prolonged adolescence; or, in my case, the adolescence I missed out on the first time around because I was so busy studying. The rite of passage, the one that I've been looking for all my life, whether it was on the docks or on Sizewell beach or some boundary I had to cross in Will Self Country, is incomplete. Will Self observes that young people use drugs as their rite of passage, the various illegal intoxicants are a slalom course between childhood and adulthood.

'Inbetween' is accepted in an anthology of rave fiction called *Disco Biscuits*. The anthology will go on to be the highest-selling anthology of short stories in British publishing history, and my story 'Inbetween' will be made into a short film. Nobody remembers *Disco Biscuits* with much fondness. It belongs to a time when the *Observer* would emblazon its masthead with the face of its star writer Will Self, announcing 'Will Self Back on Drugs'. *Trainspotting* was in the cinemas, Pot Noodle adverts were blipverts from some chill-out room; it was painful enough to think of the Nineties in the Nineties, and it is unbearable now.

I maintain a ruinous evening regime, constantly recovering from and embarking upon intoxication, falling from launch party to launch party, living high on the hog. We make a lot of noise in the back of black taxi cabs.

I try to write more fiction but I have no idea what I'm doing. Three or four pages at most before I reward myself with distraction, or work on another piece of Sponsored New Glib.

Will stays in 1 Hall Cottages for another year, writing *Great Apes*. He goes out into the marshes. Satisfied that he is alone, he begins panting and hooting, devising how the apes in his novel will communicate. Finally, with me out of the way and the cottage to himself, he is getting on with his fiction. I am obscurely offended by this; I was not an assistant in literature but an amanuensis for the New Glib, the stuff written between the novels or *the nov* as he refers to it, now that he is back on first-name terms with the form.

Will moves back to London, to a house tucked in the lee of the Westway. He is getting married and starting a new family.

He invites the Idlers to his new place in Shepherd's Bush on a Thursday night, and it's kind of a goodbye to all that, because he is moving on. My old Twirl mugs are upside down on the kitchen surface. My hair is unkempt and I am sallow-eyed. I'm holding a drink and an opinion at the same time: never a good look. My chin is streaked with the spittle of the New Glib, and I have just filed a piece called 'Not in The Real World'.

We all sit around the table. It's ten o'clock, finally we can eat. I am still talking. Will chops up a roast chicken on a wooden board, listening quietly, and then he says to me, 'Well, Matthew, what happened to that nice young man you used to be?'

Will Self's novella *The Sweet Smell of Psychosis* was published in 1996, prior to his return to the novel with *Great Apes*. The novella charts the corruption of a young provincial journalist Richard by a vile clique of the Sealink Club. The clique revolves around the *überhack* of Bell, who shares his hulking physicality with Burt Lancaster's JJ Hunsecker – the powerful opinionist at the heart of the crackling, cynical 1957 film *The Sweet Smell of Success*, the narrative template for *Psychosis*. I scour the novella for signs of myself within the character of Richard. His provincial life and corruption by the city are familiar but his condition is too generic for me to take it personally. I am representative of a generation in thrall to the big CON: Consumerism, Opportunism, Nihilism.

The *Idler* becomes infamous for its parties, holding thirty-six or so parties between the mid-Nineties and the turn of the millennium that we should regard as one long party. These bi-monthly gatherings occur in the shadow street complex of the TARDIS on Turnmill Street. Proceeds from each party are spent on improving the TARDIS for the next party, and so the

TARDIS regenerates around us as we dance.

Party proceeds allow the TARDIS to put in a proper bar, and a staircase between rooms, and a flushing toilet. George acquires a parrot. Howard continues to pursue good works under the aegis of IHAC, International Humanitarian Aid Communications, putting brand new microwave ISDN lines into Sarajevo. Howard tells me that IHAC's computers have been sabotaged in an attempt to stop their work, that Serbs bought viruses in Russia and then released them. His contact is flying in a server with the Royal Airforce.

Before one party, Howard takes me aside. He leads me into the office with its smell of old filing and smoke. Would I mind helping him with something, with part of the struggle?

'I'm trying to write a letter of introduction,' he says, working his excitable squint. He takes out an A4 pad from his desk drawer. From downstairs, the tutting *tsk tsk tsk* of house music as Andy Soundman checks the rig.

I ask Howard, 'A letter introducing you to whom?'

'Richard Branson.'

'Do you want to borrow money from him?'

'I want to borrow an airplane.' His squint runs at 120 beats per minute.

'An airplane?'

'A 747.'

I slip on one of my impassive faces. 'Why do you need a 747?'

'I'm starting an airline. Air Bosnia. I want to bring the first commercial flight into the war zone of Sarajevo.'

'What will you do once you are there?'

'Two things: first, we will distribute medicine. Secondly, we will have a party. When I was last in the city, I came across a grand old house in the centre of a minefield, and I looked around and thought: wouldn't *this* be a splendid place to have a party?'

'In a minefield?'

Howard sits in a wheeled office chair, folds one leg over the other, and kicks his heels so that he reverses quickly across the room. Reaching his desk, he turns around to pull out a folder containing his plan.

'We need a 747, my dear boy, to fly in all the guests. What better way to raise awareness about the problems caused by mines than a party in a minefield? We'll clear a path in and out of the grand old house for the partygoers. A catwalk for the models to walk down but if they stumble to the left or the right then…BOOM.' He mimes the explosion and lets out another dastardly cackle. 'BOOM…the *meeja* can experience what it's like on the ground in Sarajevo.'

He squints down at the letter. He wants my help tidying up his prose. 'Could you look at this section for me? "This is a unique opportunity to work with a leading charity and establish the first commercial flight into Sarajevo. NATO are on board and…"'

I draft a letter to Richard Branson asking to borrow a 747 so that we can fly people to a party in a grand old house in Sarajevo surrounded by a minefield. Because a war zone would be great place to have a party.

Tsk. Tsk. Tsk.

I walk out into a montage of parties. Downstairs, Lenny Beige is founding The Freedom To Party Party. I meet him on the stairs and agree to rewrite a manifesto for him too. Parties are political, aren't they? Tom asks if I can go back up to the street and help the harpist carry her instrument down three flights of stairs. I can. I lay the harp down on the sprung dancefloor. Empty sofas and standard lamps in brick archways. Andy Sound Man, pale-faced and fiddling with phono leads. Someone hands me a complimentary tinny from the bin of ice and then

I supervise the inflation of a bouncy castle in the back room, or perhaps the arrangement of a poker table, a roulette wheel, and instructions for the croupiers. From out of the walk-in safe come the cigarette girls with their platters of complimentary Camels. Brands want to be at our parties. Or at least, the people who work for brands do. On the quiet streets of Farringdon, the lamp posts and hoardings are thick with flyposters repositioning soups and snacks. Every day a new alcopop launches. Products want to be *cool* and *edgy*; even Thermos comes to us with the insistence that the flask just got hot. I work on seven things at once, always distracted, always moving on to the new new thing. Never be good at things that you hate.

The victories of the mind and spirit have to be won afresh in every age, writes the interwar intellectual Cyril Joad in his *Decadence*. The *Idler* revives arguments from Samuel Johnson and Jerome K Jerome against the Protestant work ethic, exploring a history of dissent against consumerism that is different from the worthy socialism of our elders. At the same time, triangulation makes it possible to serve the brands and marketers we loathe. But you shouldn't make a career out of cognitive dissonance; the effort in sustaining beliefs contrary to your actions will lead to a breakdown. You have to choose: Plan A or Plan B. Take the money or run. One of the symptoms of cognitive dissonance is the inability to choose.

The parties swell with notoriety. An hour or two beforehand, we sit down at KFC to discuss who is coming. Who is on the list this time. At the parties in the TARDIS, George takes Polaroid pictures of the famous and the infamous and pins them on a wall. He begins with the crooks who write books and soon the wall of Polaroids is a tapestry in which the parties merge into one long party. Pointedly, George mixes Polaroids of the TARDIS crew, the sculptors and ne'er do wells who make the place what it is, in with the famous faces. When one of the crew falls out of favour, their Polaroid is reversed and riddled with pin pricks by someone who is never discovered. I am rewarded with my own Polaroid. Howard and George forbid journalists from mentioning the TARDIS in print, as they were hardly adhering to the spirit of their lease. No gossip columnists. Total deniability. It only adds to the mystique. Parties come and go, leaving no trace. Hawaiian parties and masked balls, I'm dancing to easy listening and the sounds of pylons amplified until my trousers quiver. Howard Marks is DJ-ing again. 'The TARDIS is known to the authorities,' says one paranoid partygoer to me, 'you can rest assured that your conversations will be monitored now that Howard Marks has been here.' 'But Howard is everywhere,' I say. 'I don't think MI5 have got the manpower to follow Howard.'

The morality of the party holds sway. If we feel any responsibility or accountability outside of the big CON – consumerism, opportunism, nihilism – if we apprehend that journalism may be a force for good and not merely a platform upon which we sell generalisations formed out of our own meagre experience, then that knowledge will come to us from Gavin Hills. His schemes and plans are touched with madness and genius: Gavin is the first to spot the Spice Girls, and his friend makes a killing acquiring the rights to sell Spice Girls sticker books. If Gavin can just stay *sane*. He wanders through Glastonbury Festival dressed as King Arthur. He lives in a flat off Broadway Market in Hackney, and when El and I move into the area, he takes us to the terrace of Pub in the Park, gestures at the surrounding London Fields, and announces, 'Welcome to the Hackney Riviera.'

Gavin is 'Amnesty Journalist of the Year', reporting from war zones for the *Face*. He writes personal vignettes for the *Idler*, dispatches from his 'wonderful life', tales of his upbringing in Leatherhead and his bouts of depression. Thus he rides the blissful peaks and doom-clanging troughs of being alive, and he is oblivious to the greasy insulating caution required in dealings with our betters at the *Guardian*.

He takes to dressing up and performing rituals at the *Idler* parties. He hires a large pig suit. Along with an acolyte in a loin cloth, he waits in a side room and enacts voodoo rituals upon the guests. At the completion of the ritual, each guest is given a pill (it's aspirin). The chants of his followers echo down the shadow street and Chinese lanterns swing with the stomp of his pig legs: *voo-doo pig, voo-doo pig, voo-doo pig*. After the triumph of voodoo pig, Gavin memorises a gnostic ritual for the next party. I take my coat off and ask Gavin to perform the ritual upon me. Dressed in black silk and in elaborate hat, he intones phrases from Hermes Trismegistus. I close my eyes and give myself up to the incantation. At the end of the ritual, he asks me to fall backwards into his arms. The old trust exercise. He is there to catch me. I can feel his hands safe against my back.

The world is our oyster. An oyster is a great place to throw a party. My twenties. The Nineties. 1994: Do you want one of these? 1997: Don't you think you've had enough? I begin to avoid Will because I am failing to write. My ambition doesn't leave me, it festers. Walking into bookshops is like revisiting the site of a trauma.

Back in the montage of parties, the place is filling up. In a confession booth sit Bill Drummond and Zodiac Mindwarp. Bill was a pop star and cultural provocateur as part of the KLF, and Zodiac Mindwarp is a rock god. Together, they write the *Idler*'s Bad Advice column. In the booth, they dispense bad advice to any guests who care to wander in.

I decide to test them out.

'What ails you, my son?' asks Bill Drummond, from behind the curtain.

'Money troubles,' I say, to the man who once burned a million pounds.

Zodiac Mindwarp, in a Yorkshire brogue, says, 'If you want money, you should sell your arse.'

'Yes,' says Bill. 'Go down to Victoria station and sell your arse.'

'Don't you mean King's Cross?' I reply.

'This is bad advice,' says Bill.

The dance hall is crowded. A lean tattooed woman hangs upside down from the ceiling. She is Anglegrinder Jo. She brings her whirring tool down hard against the iron crotch of her briefs, sending sparks out over our heads. Three hundred people dancing in a room and I know everyone. Or, if not, then I know someone much like them. And then I am at the bar listening to Nick Reynolds talk about his latest art project. The son of Great Train Robber Bruce Reynolds, Nick cast the heads of the cons and the icons (his phrase) in plaster and bronze. He's always on the look out for more icons. It is due to Nick's persistence that I get Will down to the TARDIS to have his head cast. Down the alleyway where the artists work, beside the incense burners and a wrought-iron throne, amongst the squat art, Nick slathers Will's head in plaster of Paris. Will panics stoically as the mould takes, struggling to breathe through the nose holes.

Somewhere within the *Idler* party, Will stumbles on his way, the dance floor listing beneath him like the deck of a cross-Channel ferry; he doesn't know anyone here or doesn't want to know anyone, and barely recognises me when I sit next to him. His eyes are askance with intoxication, and he can't quite piece it together.

Every party is a rehearsal for the big party to come. The end of the millennium. The government-assisted end of the world. Parties lie across one another like the limbs of party goers in their 4am sprawl across the floor of my flat. I drink a beer and try to talk to Will but he can't focus upon me because time is moving too fast and I am a blur. I don't even know what year this is anymore? '95? '96? *Can anyone tell me what fucking year this is?* Anglegrinder Jo abrades the rotating blade across her iron bust, sending sparks flying to the left and to the right. I am talking about a magazine I want to start up called 'Decadence' that will begin with issue 36, then subsequent issues will count backwards so that issue 1 arrives on the first day of the new millennium. Commercialism, opportunism and nihilism. The Nineties. The CON.

Will wants to know when a young critic is going to write something serious about the novel and a survey of this decadence. He taps out a filterless Camel and looks up when I ask him if he is OK: his expression shifts between leery malevolence and innocent bewilderment. 'Oh you know me,' he says. 'I'm as paranoid and embattled as ever.'

The house lights come up. The music stops. The DJ flicks his fingernail repeatedly against the needle, and the party flinches in time, reluctant to give up their suspension of disbelief.

In between parties, I struggle to go into work. I watch X-Men cartoons before commuting reluctantly. Outside the office, a doom bell clangs so loudly in my head that I can barely speak to other people. Every night, I stumble into bed. The instant of slipping into unconsciousness jerks me awake because it feels like falling out of a tree.

A week or month later I pick up a tabloid and there is Will Self's flash-revealed, hunted face. He is accused of taking heroin on the Prime Ministerial plane while covering the general election for the *Observer* newspaper. The Tories leap on the story because they are mired in sleaze allegations made by the *Guardian*, sister paper to the *Observer*. In a distinctly moralistic election, Will Self takes a thorough rinsing in the news cycle. I guess it must be 1997 already.

On election night, 1 May, Gavin Hills holds a party in his Hackney flat, and we celebrate news of the Labour victory by letting off fireworks from the windows and from the street. Gavin is so happy that he grins from ear to ear, a wide and notorious grin that his face can barely contain.

On the morning news, Cherie Blair is filmed bleary-eyed at the door of 10 Downing Street. The morning after. A jittery low-blood sugar hangover. The party of opposition becomes the party of government. We have had our fun and now the comedown begins.

Mid-May, El and I go to London Zoo for the launch of Will Self's novel *Great Apes*. We talk to John McVicar, on hand with his dog Clem. 'This novel,' says McVicar, 'will be the one that puts Will up there with the great European novelists like Umberto Eco.' We share a cab with McVicar to the Sealink Club. At the table all the talk is about what is happening with the scandal, and what will happen to Will next. Who can he trust? *Paranoid and embattled.*

Will leans back, and says, 'Look at Matthew. He could have sold his story to the papers about me. But he kept quiet. He understands loyalty.'

I nod silently under the benediction of this compliment. I do not confess that, as a quite unnecessary young man, no newspaper has sought my side of the story. We are protective of him. I will not say a word. It's been two years since I left 1 Hall Cottages, and I am ashamed of my continuing failure to write anything other than New Glib.

At the end of May, the *Idler* is booked to perform at the Birmingham Literary Festival. Will is there too. I read out one of my *Idler* articles to a small audience. They don't get it. The article is incoherent, broken into separately titled units because I can't seem to put together a single long thought. Everything I write suffers from this incoherence. I want my work to mean so much, but that pressure of my ambition, when placed upon a rickety work ethic, results only in collapsing thought.

I proceed directly from the disappointment of my reading to interviewing Will Self on stage, armed with questions that might have made sense under the fly ceiling of 1 Hall Cottages but do not speak to the concerns of the general reader. I do not ask him about the incident on John Major's plane, so he has to take it upon himself to bring that subject up. I adopt a peculiar formality in my dealing with him, I never assume the easy manners of friendship. Part of me will always resort to the role of dutiful amanuensis.

Is obsession the architect of your recurring imagery, I ask? For William Burroughs, his fictional topography supplanted that of his lived experience; do you find that possibility of inhabiting your own fictional territory to be alluring? Somewhere, just out of my earshot, the audience cringe. You've stressed the importance of the novelist also working as a journalist so as not to be an aloof literary figure, but is journalism really preferable to the Burroughsian immersion? You have taken on the role of the satirist in the Swiftian tradition but isn't satire inherently moral, and isn't the unconscious that produces the alluring distortions and imaginative figures of your fiction entirely amoral?

It is an hour-long interview and I've shown up with five questions, each of which dwindles away under the hot discomfort of the audience. The gist was this: don't you wish you could live inside your own fiction? And because I don't have any fiction of my own, would you mind if I lived inside Will Self Country too?

I have missed the crucial fact that is blatantly obvious to everybody else. The only rite of passage for a writer is the writing of a book.

I sit outside the auditorium, head down. A lad sits next to me, my age, shaven-headed and a bit uncertain.

'I liked your story,' he says.

I don't know what he is talking about.

'Your story in *Disco Biscuits*. 'Inbetween'. I've had nights like that.' And then he goes back into the hall. It's my first encounter with a reader, and it is a marvel that I do not deserve.

After the event, we adjourn to a shared house of one of the organisers. A small terraced house, chintzy, a rented place. I sit on the floor with my friend Greg, occupied with the construction of the special cigarette. When Will arrives at the party, he greets us with an expansive 'Hel-*lo Idler* babies.'

He falls into conversation with Gavin Hills, the two of them sitting on a large shelf. Shy and high, we're content to listen to Gavin and Will's conversational flow. Toward the end of the conversation, Will says that he thinks the State is out to get him because 'I'm a fucking anarchist.' The conversation comes to an end. Will has had enough of being the centre of attention. It is exhausting to be with strangers who know who you are, who meet your casual gaze with the expectation of intimacy. Slowly Will Self gets up, shakes our hands in turn, pats me once on the back, and then he toddles off into the city in search of anonymity. I wave him goodbye, then turn back to my friends.

EPILOGUE: LITERATURE

October in 1 Hall Cottages. The day after my twenty-third birthday. I wake to the waft of the special cigarette, the smell of fresh coffee, the sound of Will at the typewriter coming from the office downstairs. I don't remember falling asleep. There is an overturned mug on the floor containing dregs of opium tea, and my own typewriter is balanced at the end of the bed, a sheet of paper half-wound around the paper cylinder. The hollow between the typewriter ribbon and the hammers smells intimately of ink, dust and oil, the body odour of a machine. I wind the paper onward and read what I hammered out when I was hammered, a self-pitying prophecy about my failure to realise my dream of becoming a writer.

I place the dour prophecy in the slim folder of my other writing. Why, in my heart, do I believe that I will not achieve my ambition? Is it something in my class upbringing, the whispers from my family that the financial risk of trying to become a writer was not for the likes of us? I had not been much of a financial burden. I had studied Creative Writing with a British Academy scholarship (Lucky, I know). Security guard work took the edge off the cost of my undergraduate living expenses. And Will is paying me a hundred quid a week with full bed and board. The source of this pessimism runs deep. It is derived from some primal disappointment I am not fully cognisant of.

The sound of typing from downstairs persists. Through the bedroom window, there is the garden and beyond that, the harvested field, yellowing leaves scattered here and there in overturned plough lines. The morning mist fills the rusted frame of the greenhouse and slides toward two empty deck chairs. In the paddock adjacent to the cottage, a horse comes out of the mist and snorts a challenge.

As I dress, I remember a dream from the night before. I'd heard voices coming from under the carpet and so I tore the top layer of carpet from its tacks, then peeled back the soft black underlay. The words 'carpet underlay' are scrawled on a Post-it note on the study wall. 'Carpet underlay' is Will Self's metaphor for the communal unconscious of the television that we have rejected in the cottage. When we move among other people, we are aware of television as their unspoken shared experience. If you do not hear music for a couple of days, you will start to dream of music; likewise, denied television, I have begun to dream of it. I peel back the underlay and think 'aha! There was a television here all along!' After wiping the screen clear, it shows a man in his early thirties in bed next to his sleeping wife, with a cot beside the bed for his new baby. The man lies awake, worrying. When he glances upward in my direction, I recognise him as myself. Either this is a prophecy or I am one of his memories, tucked away in the corner of his bedroom. 'The future enters into us,' writes Rilke, 'long before it happens.'

The morning routine. I can't remember what we used to have for breakfast apart from coffee and cigarettes. Cereal? I cannot imagine what brand of cereal could possibly be allowed in the cottage. It must have been toast. Two slices of Marmite on toast sat in a deckchair and then I clean the ashes from the grate in his study and sweep the fireplace surround, careful not to interrupt Will's hammering of typewriter keys upon the stiff white paper, the percussion of his work ethic. I clean the glasses from the night before, when we drank beer from the keg set up in the larder and then sat around the fire and gazed at the bookshelves, speculating what might happen if the characters flowed from one novel and into another, if the violent rapey homosexuals of Dennis Cooper's *Try* wandered into Cormac McCarthy's *All the Pretty Horses* to wreak havoc with the machismo of the cowboys.

In the garden, I empty the ashes into the bushes. Then I pop empty quart bottles of whisky with the air rifle.

From the cottage, the phone rings. Will lets it go to the answering machine. The content of the message is muffled but the intent is unmistakable. Someone wants Will to write something. He is writing now, always writing. He will only interrupt writing to discuss what to write next.

* * *

Rilke's *Letters to a Young Poet*, written from 1903 to 1908, were sent to an aspiring poet called Franz Xaver Kappus. They detail the selfhood required of a writer. Rilke alights upon the importance of solitude in particular. 'What is needed is this, and this alone: solitude, great inner loneliness. Going into oneself and not meeting anyone for hours – this is what one must arrive at. Loneliness of the kind one knew as a child.'

Rilke counsels Kappus to '[draw] on the depths of your own world, on the expanse of your own solitude.' The places that I remember – 1 Hall Cottages, the Dock Road, the marshlands next to the railway line where I played as a boy – were quiet and removed. Their unhurried emptiness moved into me, becoming the solitude necessary for writing. As an amanuensis, I was under no pressure to shape my own life. The future was patient. In my spare time, I returned to the solitude of childhood, fascinated by the surfaces of things, and ignorant of their deeper laws. I had time to crouch beside the breaking surf at Sizewell Beach and feel its every happening; Dictaphone in hand, I recorded the sound of the waves breaking and fancied that I heard a grammar in their exclamatory arrival and whispering withdrawal.

I couldn't be alone in my twenties, and so I did not write fiction. Cyril Connolly was clear on the question of solitude: 'a writer who is not prepared to be lonely in his youth must if he is to succeed face loneliness in his middle age.' Now, while I am a domestic family man, I am no longer social. The question is whether the days I spend writing constitute solitude. Fleetingly. The word 'solitude' is the fossil of a feeling that is mostly extinct. In writing this memoir, I've tried to retain the innocence of my younger self to recover one or two of the lost emotions of the pre-digital age. One of these is solitude, the other is a feeling of specialness around my upbringing.

On the landing of the house where I grew up, there was (and still is) a white-painted metal banister that runs alongside the staircase like a long thin ski-slope. At the top of the slope, the banister turns into a rail. As a three-year old child, I would sit at the top of the stairs and play with the cold rail and banister. My solitude was structured by it. There is gap of about five centimetres between the bottom of the rail and the carpet, just wide enough to fit a toy car. Returning to the banister forty years later, I realise that whoever installed it did a botch job; instead of securing the rail to the floorboard, it floats free, hence the gap. As a child I thought that this banister was the only possible banister, that my family was the only significant family. (One of the rarer definitions of solitude in the *Oxford English Dictionary* is the condition of being sole or unique.) The aura around childhood objects – the fug of the airing cupboard, the ridged patterns of the linoleum floor, the head of the nail under the thick gloss paint of the skirting board – is generated by an ignorant belief in specialness. I suppose you could call it innocence.

The urge to write may begin with innocent delusion but it does not stay that way for long, if you write with your eyes open. Writers are pragmatic in ways that they are rarely given credit for. Unlike middle managers and bureaucrats, writers take responsibility for what they have created. The passive voice, beloved of the elite, in which mistakes were made and lessons must be learned, effaces who did what. Writers work in the active voice. We carry the can. In a society of perpetual beta, we finish what we have started and then stand or fall by it.

You want to be a writer because the act of writing concentrates your thought; as your style gains in precision and clarity, so do you. Acts of attentiveness gather together the fragments of your self. Books are zones of focus in a landscape of distraction. You want to be a writer because you walk around all day jingling words and phrases in your pockets like loose change, making nonsense rhythms, unexpected aphorisms. Because you think in dialogue, talking to what Will Self calls 'the imaginary interlocutor', your lips moving silently across both sides of a daydream conversation as you sit on the train, on the way to work.

When I lived with Will, I wanted to be a writer. Now that I am middle-aged, I just want to write. I am ambivalent toward the social role of *the writer* which only encourages my narcissism. The fantasy of being a writer gets in the way of the writing.

There: I've kept that habit acquired in the cottage of talking about 'the writing' rather than 'my writing'. It was never about self-expression. We wanted to take dictation, the ideas already out there, pre-existing in the world, waiting for us to uncover them.

My interest in writing encompasses every aspect of my life; when I am not writing, then I'm reading or teaching creative writing at a university. Will Self has written and spoken against the teaching of creative writing; on this matter, we disagree. I believe that students should be taught to write fiction. It cultivates attentiveness to the people around them, their motivations and inner worlds, the work they read, the possibilities of language, the arbitrary construction of the culture they inhabit. The writer and academic Professor Marina Warner writes that, 'Creative writing teaches attentiveness to the qualities of a text, to its structure and latent meanings. Such developed linguistic capacity can help us to counter the codes and systems and protocols that increasingly regiment our world.'

In the cottage, writing was a way of exposing the absurdity of the given world. In the Nineties, there was still a sense that power was listening to writers. Now, literature is more a consolation for the increasing majority of the left behind, the ones who care, who notice, who feel, who know, who are accountable: literature is for the losers, basically. Established writers may bemoan the novel's loss of centrality to our culture but maybe that position required a complicity with power that it should no longer perform. When power admits no accountability to literature, that tells you more about the changed nature of power than it does about literature.

Studying creative writing was the only way I knew to get out of one life and start imagining another. I have used books like a dope addict, to return to the quote from Saul Bellow that is one of this memoir's epigrams. I was a user of books, my reading a gnawing search for something that would tell me how to live and how to be in the world. I read impatiently and ambitiously. Aristotle said that a man is his desire. Chekhov wrote something similar: 'Tell me what you want and I will tell you what manner of man you are.' My ambition to be writer, finally fulfilled in the act of writing, made me into *this*.

In his essay, 'Why Bother?' Jonathan Franzen discusses the research of Shirley Brice Heath, a linguistic anthropologist from Stanford. From her interviews with readers of substantive literature, she identifies its audience as people who have left behind their social and cultural origins, their lives going down a different path from the one they were born to walk. Literature is read by people in the process of creating a new identity, leaving behind an old one for reasons concerned with gender, race, class or cultural preference. Novels give us access to other lives, a few of which might be our own. Literary ambition belongs to readers as well as writers.

Ambition forces us to choose between who we were and who we might become. Choice is at the heart of conventional dramatic structure, invariably the agonising choice of the protagonist, or a decision made in haste or unwittingly, with consequences unfolding across the story. The novel is an outgrowth of the mind's ability to imaginatively model the consequences of our actions; when faced with a difficult choice, we devise scenarios, place ourselves within them, to discover which potential life we could most easily bear.

The philosopher Daniel Dennett refers to stories as 'intuition pumps'; that is, stories constitute a culture's sense of what is natural. Stories are the tracks upon which we run. In the cottage, we never really bothered thinking about stories, as they seemed synonymous with the delusions of literary realism. 'Stories are a bore,' observes William Gass. 'Story is what you do to clean up life and make God into a good burgher who manages the world like a business... stories deny that life is no more than an endlessly muddled middle, they beg each length of it to have a beginning and end like a ballgame or a banquet.' The Nineties was more interested in style than story, and I think this approach was a dead end. As Geoff Dyer knowingly observes, 'Don't be one of those writers who sentence themselves to a lifetime of sucking up to Nabokov.' Literature may have been pushed out of the power party but it is more engaged with suffering, injustice and kindness.

In Will Self's interview with Adam Phillips, the critic and psychoanalyst emphasised the role of stories in forming our identity. Breaking out of dysfunctional patterns was a matter of telling a new story. 'The understanding of any single emotion,' writes the American philosopher Martha Nussbaum, 'is incomplete unless its narrative history is grasped and studied for the light it sheds on the present response.' Our emotions are part-now, part-buried secret coming back to the surface. Will attributed the intensity of his present feeling to his past troubles. The return of something buried, how the past is disinterred by the present, is a deep pattern of story going all the way back to Oedipus discovering the secret of his parentage. Storytelling is both more difficult and instrumental than I realised.

What do I teach? Good writing should induce a continuous dream in the reader; this prescription comes from John Gardner, novelist and influential teacher of creative writing.

He advises trimming infelicities of style that might interrupt a reader's immersion in your work. (John Gardner would not have approved of Will Self's arcane vocabulary, the obscure words that rear out of the water to puncture the hull of the complacent reader.) Gardner's continuous dream is not only for readers. It also suggests the zone the writer longs to inhabit, a Möbius strip in which the illusion of two sides – writing or not writing – is in fact one continuous strip of writing and dreaming about writing.

This question – why write – has to be answered by each generation. I have my answer, my faith. But I understand that my inchoate faith will not be shared by my students. I cannot hope to convert them merely through sermon. It requires acts of observance: weekly exercises, the reading of literature, studies in story structure and narrative technique, the many possible forms and approaches to their work. I scan their faces, wondering what they think of this twentieth-century man with his talk of the novel and his long reading list and his tweedy code of a writer's discipline and attentiveness.

I help the students discover the routines and ways of seeing that lead to a creative act. If I can only help them inhabit the zone of attentiveness. If I can only teach them how not to be boring. Distraction is hell, I say. Sustained attention upon one thing that you read or write from beginning to end will change you. No act of remembering is too trivial, I think, if it calls to mind within the reader something fleetingly realised but subsequently forgotten. A few of the students, slyly checking their phones under the desk, glance up at me, wondering: does he know what he sounds like?

I have faith in literature. There, I said it. I am a believer. I am Sid Literary Bonkers. The novel is my particular sect. I believe in the novel because you don't need a million pounds to create one. I believe in its intimacy. I believe in its superior technology, that is, its language. I believe in the ingenuity and originality of a form that reflects content. I believe the novel can be a moral good even if it describes the vilest acts.

Literature is my transcendental signifier, a term I picked up from half-reading Derrida. On my initial half-reading, I thought the transcendental signifier was a good thing: the ultimate referent that exists outside of other sources of meaning or signification, a foundation that makes meaning possible, like God or the Jungian collective unconscious or what interwar mystics would call 'the Absolute'. Something above the given world that suffuses it with meaning yet remains unprovable.

To Derrida, the transcendental signifier was a bad thing; he argued that the transcendental signifier propped up dominant ideological discourse; without the foundation of the transcendental signifier, all possible meanings are in play, each with no greater claim than any other. I accept that all I can offer is faith and not proof. A faith in literature is what I wave my hand at when I am asked why I bother with all that reading and that writing.

By *literature* I mean the acts of reading and writing that have a value regardless of the economic imperatives of publishing; literature can happen in the form of poetry or science fiction, literary fiction or graphic novels. In one way, the argument for literature is easier to make than it used to be, back when my old schoolmates, confronted with another excerpt from *Hamlet*, would ask of my English teacher, 'But, Sir, how will knowing about Shakespeare help me get a job in the real world?'

The real world as I once knew it – a reliable substrate of blue collar labour and common sense – has broken up and floated off like melting glaciers. We live our half-lives inside a smartphone, spending funny money and caught up in the political fantasies of a dying order. No wonder so many us want to be writers. Given the imaginary quality of everyday life, dreaming is a pragmatic response.

* * *

For many years, I held down a media job and wrote in my spare time. I wrote one novel that way.

On reading through a draft of my first novel, I realised what was wrong with it: I was not a good enough person to write a good novel. Bad writing is a ruthless exposure of the writer, and it is made all the more painful because the writer is unaware of how carelessly their psychological baggage has been loaded onto the page. Rewriting my novel was also a redrafting of my self. Cutting away snark in my depiction of minor characters, trying to think my way into other points of view, was a kind of moral hygiene. Other people have never been my strong point.

After the first novel was published, I tried to write a second novel. But I had a young family and a demanding job. I was too distracted. It was around this time that Will treated me to a meal in Chinatown. He was writing *Umbrella*, a novel without paragraph and chapter breaks, his response to Modernism. I reminded him that twenty years ago, in the Chequers pub, he had mooted a novel called *Untitled* that was stripped of all the armature of the physical text, and here he was, finally writing it. That the intent to write a novel like *Umbrella* existed in nascent form twenty years previously was, at first, kind of shocking. But the more we thought about it, the more it made sense. You think you are progressing through life, but in your work, you are really looping back and forth in time and mind.

After dinner, I stood on the corner of the Strand, talking out my writing problems with Will as he unhooked his bicycle from a railing. He listened to me kvetch about writing, zipped up his windcheater, and turned an idle circle on his bike, as ascetic and idly ruthless as a praying mantis.

'You have to step up, Matthew,' he said, pedalling out into traffic. 'Step up' as in to step up to the plate, a baseball expression for that moment when it is your turn to act. I tried to protest but he called back to me, 'STEP UP!'

Will Self's *Umbrella* moves associatively through minds and across time. Sentences break off in the interior monologue of a woman, Audrey De'Ath, in an interwar hospital and resume in the mind of a psychoanalyst, Dr Zack Busner, treating her decades later. Busner is a recurring character in Will Self's novels; he is the RD Laing-like originator of the Quantity Theory of Insanity, and he cameos in various short stories and novels. With *Umbrella*, Busner moves centre-stage, becoming the consciousness that holds the novel and its two sequels together. Busner moves from being the object of satire in the early short stories into a rich subjectivity in which intellectual riffs are underscored by grief, loss, physical decline and memories of desire. The emotional range of *Umbrella* is broader than an earlier novel such as *How the Dead Live*. The shift of Busner from the subject of satire to its source tracks Will Self's evolving identification with his media shrink.

Umbrella is a response to the literary movement of Modernism and the trauma of the First World War, remaking the formal and lexical invention devised by writers of that period. Under the influence of Freud's psychoanalytical method, Darwin's theory of evolution, and Einstein's theory of general relativity, combined with technological innovation such as telephony, the internal combustion engine and powered flight, our understanding of time, space and consciousness changed, and literature changed accordingly. Writers such as James Joyce and Virginia Woolf adopted the technique of stream of consciousness as way of infolding the fleeting and intimate impression of thought upon the page.

In the novel, time can be manipulated more adroitly than in other mediums. A skilful writer can slip a reader between the past and the future without them noticing. Stream of consciousness – influenced by the philosopher Henri Bergson, who described mind and time as constituting a continuous flow of reality – breaks away from conventional linear time for something more fluid. It can slow time so that every fleeting instant is recorded – I think of Giacometti's sketches of city streets, furiously trying to capture the flux of modern life – and it can rearrange time according to the loose associations of memory, as with Proust's *À La Recherche du Temps Perdu*, the volumes of which Will Self bound in cardboard and lugged around when travelling as a young man.

Most of Will Self's novels have a close relationship with another text. *The Sweet Smell of Psychosis* adapted the title and structure of the cynical 1957 movie *The Sweet Smell of Success; Great Apes* leaps off from the species inversion of *Planet of the Apes; Dorian* updates Oscar Wilde's novel *The Picture of Dorian Gray* to depict gay life under the shadow of AIDS; *The Book of Dave* is the closest Will Self comes to science fiction, imagining a flooded Britain in which the inhabitants speak a future language influenced by Russell Hoban's 1980 novel *Riddley Walker*. The trilogy of novellas that comprise *Walking to Hollywood* are Will Self's response to the digressive and ambulatory novels of WG Sebald, right down to interspersing the text with obscure photographs. Each novel creates its own canon, responding and reacting against what has already been written. With *Umbrella*, he steps up to the big one, James Joyce's *Ulysses*.

In a Chinese restaurant, taking a break from the pains of writing *Umbrella*, Will demonstrated to me over and again how his main character Audrey De'Ath operated a lathe. Audrey makes shells for the war on the production line but at the same time, her mind is being shaped through its subordination to the operation of the machine.

Also interwoven in the novel is the experience of her two brothers: Stanley is caught up in the First World War, and – in a fantastic set piece – she dreams of him entering an underground community of soldiers in no-man's land; meanwhile her other brother Albert, a bureaucratic savant, presides over the absurd inhumanity of military bureaucratic logic.

Describing *Umbrella* to me, doubt surfaced in Will's face, the fear that no-one would read it, that it would be declared too difficult or self-indulgent and be ignored. Nabokov calls this doubt 'the monster of grim commonsense' that must be shot dead when the author sits down to write.

Umbrella was a triumph. It was short-listed for the Booker Prize and marked a new phase in Will Self's work: two subsequent novels, *Shark* and *Phone*, took the story further into twentieth- and twenty-first-century history, completing a trilogy concerned with madness, war and technology. His archive has been acquired by the British Library, an indication that his books will be here for the long haul.

The *New Statesman* headlined their review of *Phone* with 'One of the most significant literary works of our century'. The second sequel to *Umbrella*, its military strand takes in the British involvement in the invasion of Iraq. Horrors take place during an expedition by the troops to secure some white garden chairs. Joseph Heller's *Catch-22* is a strong and self-admitted influence on Will Self, ever since he read and re-read the novel twelve times when he was a teenager. Heller's tone and comic extrapolations in the face of war's horrors are a 'veritable manual of satire', and they are pressed into service in finding the tone of the British military action in Iraq: not so much the heart of darkness as the heart of debacle.

In the novel, the then-Prime Minister Tony Blair becomes TeeBee. The initialising of his name recalls the coercive informality of Blair's Third Way. Under his premiership, the leaders of institutions sought to square self-interest and social good, to triangulate their way across contraries, to offer up ideas and visions in the place of policy. Also, TeeBee because the military encode reality within acronyms.

In May 2003, Tony Blair addressed the British troops in Basra. Jacket off, tie off, cuffs rolled back, he looked like he was motivating staff to pull a long weekend at the office and not ranks of soldiers wearing desert fatigues. This was the true end of the Nineties; the party that became a war.

As for me, I took Will's advice and stepped up. I'd waited my whole life to do it. I left my job and raced to complete my second novel before my savings ran out. But my first attempt to step up was in vain. My novel went bad. It hadn't been raised right. My agent shook her head. Not even fit to submit to publishers, and consigned to my bottom drawer.

Terence Blacker, the writer who introduced me to Will when I was a student, observed that real writers have at least one novel in a drawer. So I took the failure as a good sign. I wrote and published a history of camping instead, and then embarked upon a third novel that was so ambitious that I really didn't know if I could write it. Without a publisher or job, I often ran out of money while working on this novel but I kept faith, and so did my family, and I was lucky. It was published, and so was my next one.

My novels are science fiction. Science fiction started out as pulp modernism. Not experimental like the Modernists in terms of form or style but modern in its desire to restore a transcendent aura to a life without god. Science fiction has its hack work, its genre conventions but at its best it evokes the sublimity of the universe and possible worlds. It turns away from the given world to look to the future, transforming the known with an imperious hypothesis: *what if?* It models the consequences of that question on a humanity-wide scale.

It is also escapist.

Or, to put it less childishly, science fiction is a genre in which I can imagine possibilities beyond the constraints of the given world. Will Self's early satirical stories and novels take a similar pleasure in slipping the conventions of the possible and the consensus of the real, only to double back and hold the edifice of everyday complicity up for ruthless inspection. Sometimes science fiction does that too, sometimes it keeps going and doesn't look back.

In science fiction, I can fly. We all hope to transcend – quoting Chekhov – 'a stunted, wingless life'. There is a devastating passage in Saul Bellow's novel *Humboldt's Gift* that describes how the acceptance of a position in bourgeois life comes at the cost of flight, that is, the fantasy of unlimited potential. 'People rich in abilities, in sexual feeling, rich in mind and in invention – all the highly gifted see themselves shunted for decades onto dull sidings, banished exiled nailed up in *chicken coops*.'

The italics are mine.

I had allowed myself to be distracted by an 'arrested, adolescent will-to-omnipotentiality' (Will Self's phrase), the belief that I could do anything if I tried. I was a young man who compared the books I read with the books in my head, and found them wanting. There is a great line in Jenny Offill's *Dept. of Speculation* in which a young man, sounding off at a party, is chastised by the older generation, 'You are not allowed to compare your imagined accomplishments to our actual ones.'

I take more pleasure in reading now, and tend to admire writers rather than cavil about their work. Reading a novel like *Phone*, I believe in its unexpected junctions of intimacy and sympathy. Will once taught me the Freudian term 'polymorphously perverse', meaning our ability to experience sensual pleasure from any part of the body. *Phone* is polymorphously reasonable; that is, it reaches out through florid phantasmogoria but brings us back to a sane reckoning concerned with death and kindness.

Acts of kindness are rarely entered into history's ledger. Literature corrects this, recording secret selves, common feeling, and our abiding resistance to the way the world is presented to us. I am not saying that writers are saints. Everything I write is bound up with my failings. This memoir is a kind of betrayal too, even if its intention is the opposite. I just wanted to remember what the past felt like, and to save something from long ago that matters to me.

One final memory from the beginning of my life. There was a morning, when I was three years old, when I realised that I could not fly. The frustration was like the thrashing of a lost tail. I had clear memories of flying free yet I was earthbound. My dreams had fooled me. They were so convincingly underwritten by the muscle memory of weightless drifting in the womb.

That morning, gripping the bars of the banister rail, trying to levitate, I realised that the reality principle had me by the ankles. Downstairs, the porch door rattled, my grandfather had come to collect me. I wanted to see him but walking down the stairs took so long.

I let go of the cold metal bars of the rail and drifted down the staircase. Turning heels over head, I floated into the living room, right into the corner where the wall met the ceiling. There I saw my grandfather remove his gloves, smooth the strands of hair upon his pate, ready to take me to nursery.

Memory stitches together dream and reality. All my birdmen; I never understood what they were trying to tell me until now. A hybrid of the mundane and the transcendent, the birdman is a vision of adulthood in which the imaginary is not discarded after a rite of passage but incorporated, becoming half of your self.

STEP UP! Up, up, and away!

ACKNOWLEDGMENTS

I owe a substantial debt to Will for many things, not least his generosity, which began on the first day of our friendship. One day someone will write the full story of his life. Maybe it will be him.

I wrote a first draft of *Self & I* as an escape from the painful experience of having a novel on submission with publishers, and to help my students. It is dedicated to anyone who wants to write fiction, is trying to write fiction, or has written fiction and is trying to find their way back to it.

That *Self & I* survived my dithering is due to the faith shown by my agent Sarah Such and editor Scott Pack. I first met Sarah when I was working for Will and she was a publicist for Penguin. She was rather fabulous and accompanied us on a book tour. Years later, when she was setting up as a literary agent, she accepted me as one of her first clients. Sarah is one of many people present in this time period only to have been omitted by me from this memoir.

I considered replacing these acknowledgments with a list of apologies to various people who were *there* but are not *here*, but the list was too long. A general apology to people will have to suffice. I apologise for leaving you out of certain scenes. I apologise for not giving a full and frank account of your more central contribution. I've tried to be discreet and work around people who aren't writers and so are not complicit with this act of making personal experience public. I know that you are not really Doris Literary Bonkers. I know that you are not really El. I'd like to say sorry to the pheasant; we both know that it didn't quite go down like that. The person I appear to be in this memoir is different from the man I am now. The same is true of Will, I'm certain.

It was the publication of an initial extract in *Five Dials* magazine that led to this fuller account and for that I thank Craig Taylor, Anna Kelly and Simon Prosser.

Thanks also to Tom and Gavin at the *Idler*, who gave me a chance.

This book owes its farce to Bruce Robinson's *Withnail and I*. I thought it was also inspired by Nicholson Baker's *U & I*, but I read that book a long time ago at 1 Hall Cottages, and only half-remember it, so maybe that's a red herring. Thanks to Matt Thorne who read a late draft and gave me vital feedback, half of which I've ignored, because I'm a fool to myself.

Love and gratitude to my wife Cathy. Love always to my children Alice, Alfred and Florence. Love and respect to my father Eddie.

Thanks to Anindita Basu Sempere for the beautiful translation of the line from Amiel's *Journal Intime*: 'Un paysage quelconque est un état de l'âme' rendered as 'A landscape, then, is a state of the soul, and whoever knows how to read both is astonished to find likenesses across every detail.'

Matthew De Abaitua,
Hackney, 2018